DEBATE Pro

Book 6

Author Jonathan S. McClelland
- BA in English with a Writing Concentration, University of South Carolina, Columbia, SC, USA
- Former English instructor at Daewon Foreign Language High School
- Current debate instructor for elementary school students
- Former curriculum developer at Korean Army Intelligence School
- Expert test developer of TOEFL, TOEIC, and TEPS

DEBATE Pro Book 6

Publisher Chung Kyudo
Editors Hong Inpyo, Cho Sangik
Proofreader Michael A. Putlack
Designers Zo Hwayoun, Park Sunyoung

First Published in August 2014
By Darakwon, Inc.
Darakwon Bldg., 211, Munbal-ro, Paju-si, Gyeonggi-do 10881
Republic of Korea
Tel: 82-2-736-2031 (Ext. 250)
Fax: 82-2-732-2037

Copyright © 2014 Darakwon, Inc.

All rights reserved. No part of this publication may be reproduced, stored in a retrieval system, or transmitted in any form or by any means, electronic, mechanical, photocopying or otherwise, without the prior consent of the copyright owner. Refund after purchase is possible only according to the company regulations. Contact the above telephone number for any inquiries. Consumer damages caused by loss, damage, etc. can be compensated according to the consumer dispute resolution standards announced by the Korea Fair Trade Commission. An incorrectly collated book will be exchanged.

ISBN 978-89-277-0742-4 58740
978-89-277-0677-9 58740 (set)

www.darakwon.co.kr

Components Main Book / Workbook
13 12 11 10 9 8 7   24 25 26 27 28

Instilling Knowledge and Skills
for Thoughtful Debate

DEBATE Pro

Book 6

Preface

The *Debate Pro* series is designed to provide students with an intermediate EFL ability with a sound understanding of a variety of debate topics and develop their speaking, listening, and critical thinking skills through debate. The series consists of eight sets of books, each of which includes a Main Book and a Workbook. Each Main Book includes five chapters covering five debate skills. Within each chapter, there are two units which each cover different topics for a total of ten debate topics per book. The Workbook supplements the Main Book by helping students understand the topic more deeply, developing skills for making examples and doing research, and evaluating the debates. The Workbook can be used in class and for homework assignments.

In the book, every debate topic is introduced with a large color photograph relating to the topic. Students are asked to analyze the picture and formulate opinions about the topic through a series of six warm-up questions. The topic is then explained in more detail through a reading passage of about 300 words which briefly presents background information about the topic before outlining arguments in favor of and against the topic. The passages are followed by vocabulary and comprehension exercises. Students are then required to apply what they have learned from the passage to answer a series of in-depth questions relating to the debate topic. Following these questions, students are given opinion examples before learning the debate skill for each topic. Finally, students will have the chance to apply their knowledge to create a full debate with the assistance of sample arguments and a debate flow chart.

Each book provides free MP3 files with recordings of the reading passages and opinion examples for every unit. There is also a Teacher's Guide available at www.darakwon.co.kr that includes answer keys and sample answers for every unit as well as teaching tips and suggestions for supplementing the material.

The *Debate Pro* series has the following features:

- Ten different debate topics per book covering a range of themes including education, technology, relationships, and responsibility
- Reading passages which provide a general understanding of arguments both for and against the given topic
- Questions that require students to formulate arguments and supporting opinions about each topic
- Five different debate skills per book designed to improve students' critical thinking and speaking skills
- Sample opinions and argument examples which help students develop their own arguments
- Free MP3 files with recordings of all passages and sample opinions

Contents

About This Book _7

Chapter 1
Organizing Supporting Arguments

Unit 01 Restricting Mass Tourism _12
Unit 02 Privatizing Education _22

Chapter 2
Developing Logical Supporting Reasons

Unit 03 Talking on Cell Phones on Public Transportation _34
Unit 04 Banning Bottled Water _44

Chapter 3
Developing Effective Supporting Reasons

Unit 05 Returning Art Stolen during Wars _56
Unit 06 Single-Gender Schools _66

Chapter 4
Giving Supporting Examples

Unit 07 Celebrities Having No Right to Privacy _78
Unit 08 Replacing Textbooks with Tablets _88

Chapter 5
Doing Research

Unit 09 Fat Tax on Unhealthy Foods _100
Unit 10 Banning Homework at Schools _110

About This Book

Overview

Debate Pro main book consists of five chapters. Each chapter contains two units with each focusing on the same debate skill. Every unit is further subdivided into part A and part B. Part A, Learning about the Topic, introduces students to the topic of the unit and consists of approximately one hour of learning material. Part B, Debating the Topic, requires students to formulate their arguments and debate the topic of the unit. The total time required for Part B is also approximately one hour.

Introduction for each section

Warm-up

This part includes a picture related to the topic for students to analyze. The pictures are followed by six warm-up questions. The questions in Part A require students to analyze the picture and can be answered as a class. In Part B, students draw upon their knowledge about the topic to answer questions with a partner.

Reading Passage

This part consists of a single reading passage approximately 300 words in length. The passage introduces general background information about the topic and presents specific arguments with examples both in favor of and against the topic.

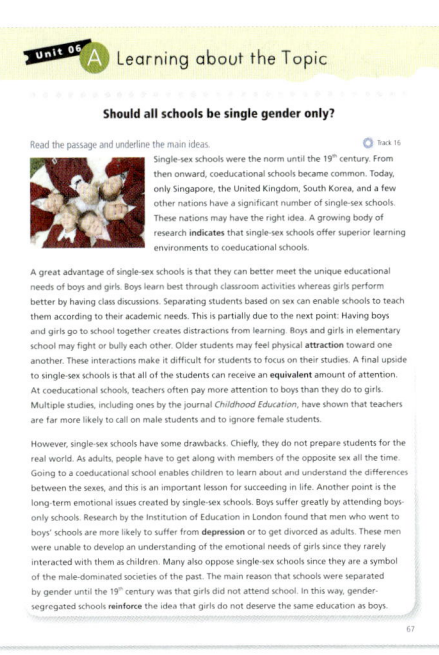

Vocabulary Check

Each reading passage is followed by five vocabulary questions to bolster students' vocabulary and ensure their understanding of the passage.

Comprehension Questions

Each reading passage includes four paired-choice reading comprehension questions. The questions ask students about the main idea of passage, factual information, and reasoning from the passage.

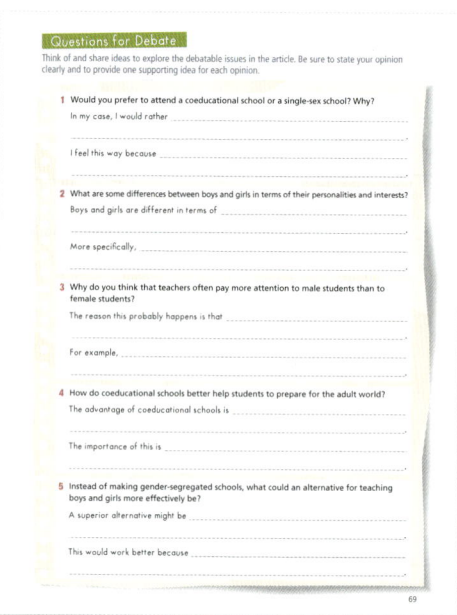

Questions for Debate

This portion consists of five open-ended questions related to the topic. The students must formulate opinions about each question and give reasons for their opinions. Key phrases are provided to help students improve their speaking skills.

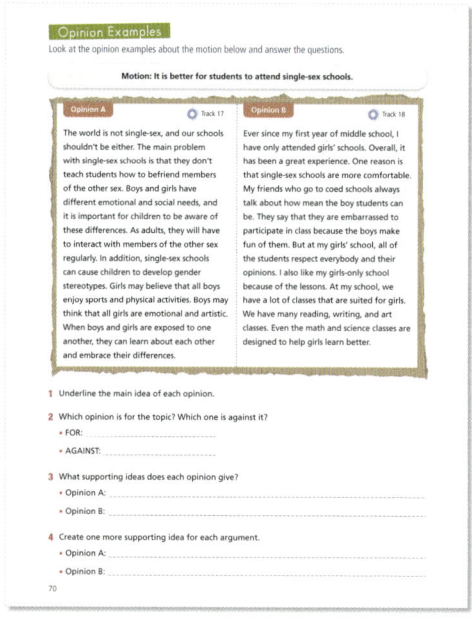

Opinion Examples

In this section, two opinion examples for and against the topic are provided. Students are required to understand the main idea of each example opinion and its supporting arguments. They must also provide an additional argument for each opinion.

Skills for Debate

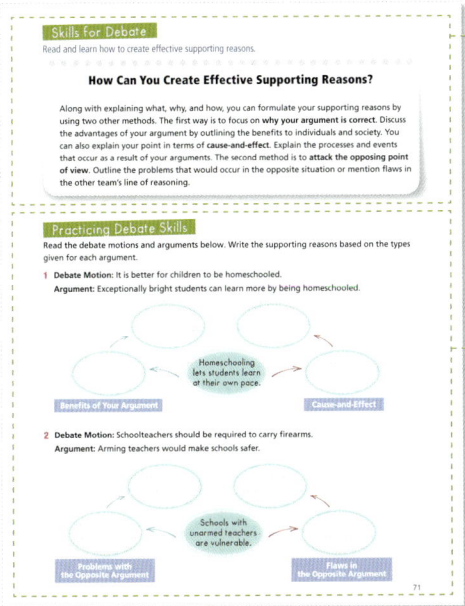

This section introduces a debate skill and explains key concepts related to the topic. Each chapter focuses on a single debate skill across two units.

Practicing Debate Skills

This exercise follows each debate skill explanation to ensure that students understand the skill and can use it during their debate.

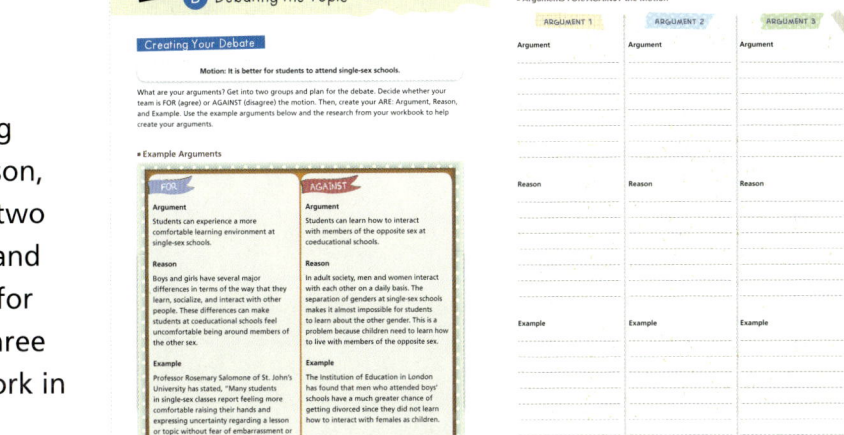

Creating Your Debate

This section begins by introducing the skills of ARE: Argument, Reason, and Example. Following this are two sample arguments, one for PRO and one for CON, with sample notes for the ARE. On the next page are three blank columns for students to work in teams and create their AREs.

Actual Debate

This portion consists of a debate flow chart. The chart outlines the order of debate and provides sample phrases to help students use proper debate language.

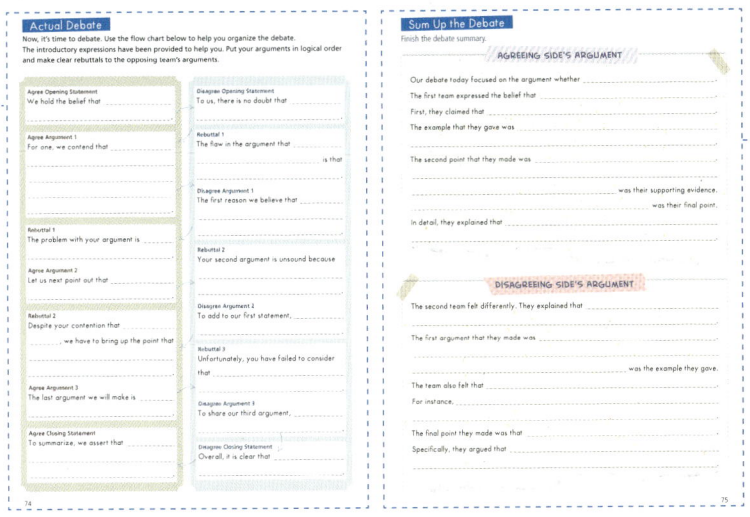

Sum Up the Debate

The final section requires students to summarize the arguments presented by both the PRO and CON teams during the debate. Sample phrases are given to help students.

Chapter 1

Organizing Supporting Arguments

Unit 01 Restricting Mass Tourism

Unit 02 Privatizing Education

Unit 01 Restricting Mass Tourism

A. Discuss the following questions as a class.
1. What do you see in the picture above?
2. Based on the clothing the people are wearing, where do you think they are going to visit?
3. How could traveling on an airplane be bad for the environment?

B. Answer the following questions with a partner.
1. Where are some places that you and your family have taken a vacation?
2. What are some activities that people do on vacation that can damage the environment?
3. Do you think people pay less attention to the environment when they are on vacation?

Unit 01   A   Learning about the Topic

Should mass tourism be restricted in order to protect nature?

Read the passage and underline the main ideas.

Tourism is one of the biggest businesses in the world. It is estimated that the tourism industry comprises 6 percent of the global economy with nearly one billion people vacationing each year. Many of these people vacation in parks, on beaches, and in other **fragile** ecosystems. Considering the massive scale of the tourism industry, it should come as no surprise that tourism results in undesirable side effects. These consequences offer good reasons to put an end to mass tourism.

The most obvious drawback to mass tourism is the physical impact caused by development. The construction of hotels, restaurants, **recreational** facilities, and sewage systems for tourists involves many environmentally destructive activities. These include sand mining, soil erosion, and widespread paving. Furthermore, the tourists themselves present a great threat to the environment. They create huge amounts of waste that destroy the environment. For instance, in the Caribbean Sea, tourist cruise ships generate 77 percent of ship waste. On average, the passengers on cruise ships produce 3.5 kilograms of waste each day compared to the 0.8 kilograms of trash that local citizens produce. Finally, mass tourism has negative social effects. Tourism creates an **awkward** relationship between visitors and locals. Some visitors expect the locals to serve them, often causing the locals to feel **hostile** towards outsiders. This results in poor relationships between travelers and local residents.

Even so, there are many valid arguments to keep the tourism industry going. Primarily, tourism is a great source of income. For developing nations, tourists from wealthy countries make substantial contributions to the local economy. A good example of this is Bangkok, Thailand. The city hosts around 16 million visitors per year. These visitors spend more than $15 billion dollars annually and greatly boost the national economy of Thailand. It must also be noted that tourism is becoming more environmentally friendly. Sustainable tourism refers to the development of tourism areas that do not harm local environments. The **aim** of such tourism is to maintain natural areas so that future generations may enjoy them. Last, but not least, tourism can expose people to various places and cultures. By visiting other nations, people can become more respectful and tolerant of individuals who are different.

Vocabulary Check

Choose the correct word for each definition.

> fragile   recreational   awkward   hostile   aim

1 the purpose or intent of something   _____
2 not friendly   _____
3 not easy to deal with   _____
4 easily broken or damaged   _____
5 done for enjoyment   _____

Comprehension Questions

Check the correct answer for each question.

1 What is true about both parks and beaches?
   ☐ They are unusual vacation destinations.
   ☐ They are ecosystems damaged by tourism.

2 What are some of the environmental problems brought on by the creation of tourist facilities? Choose TWO correct answers.

   ☐ Wearing away soil   ☐ Creating large mines
   ☐ Laying down pavement   ☐ Polluting drinking water

3 Why might some people living in tourist areas feel angry toward visitors?
   ☐ Because some tourists expect the locals to wait on them
   ☐ Because the tourists throw away too much garbage

4 How does sustainable tourism address the shortcomings of traditional tourism?
   ☐ It provides a great boost to the local economies of popular tourist areas.
   ☐ It preserves the natural environment in order to maintain its structure.

Questions for Debate

Think of and share ideas to explore the debatable issues in the article. Be sure to state your opinion clearly and to provide one supporting idea for each opinion.

1. Whenever you go on vacation, do you show concern for the local environment? Explain.

   During my vacations, I _____

   _____.

   To clarify my point, consider that _____

   _____.

2. Do you think that people are more likely or less likely to pollute when they are on vacation?

   I believe that _____

   _____.

   I feel this way because _____

   _____.

3. Do you think the economic benefits of mass tourism offset the problems caused to the environment?

   I am convinced that _____

   _____.

   For example, _____

   _____.

4. What are some ways that governments can reduce the environmental damage caused by tourism?

   It would be possible for them to _____

   _____.

   Consider that _____

   _____.

5. How do local citizens probably feel when they are forced to interact with tourists all the time?

   My feeling is that _____

   _____.

   My reasoning is _____

   _____.

Opinion Examples

Look at the opinion examples about the motion below and answer the questions.

> **Motion: Mass tourism should be restricted in order to protect nature.**

Opinion A Track 02

Going on vacation is no more harmful than living your daily life. This is why I think the idea of banning tourism is silly. Sure, building hotels and restaurants damages the natural environment, but human beings will affect the natural environment no matter where they go. We might as well allow tourism so that people can be happy. In addition, we cannot overlook the economic benefits of tourism. For many developing countries, tourism is a huge source of income. If tourism were banned, then millions of people around the world would lose their jobs. The impact to their quality of life would be far greater than the damage that tourists cause to the environment.

Opinion B Track 03

It is always fun to travel to faraway places but not if it destroys the environment. This is why mass tourism should be put to an end. Chiefly, tourists create too much garbage. They produce lots of trash and litter wherever they want. This can severely damage fragile ecosystems such as forests and beaches. And let's not forget the facilities for tourists. Just visit any tourist resort in Thailand or Indonesia, and you will see dozens of huge hotels, restaurants, and shops. Building these ruins the natural landscape of these delicate ecosystems, and these facilities continue to be major sources of pollution long after they are constructed.

1 Underline the main idea of each opinion.

2 Which opinion is for the topic? Which one is against it?
- FOR: _____
- AGAINST: _____

3 What supporting ideas does each opinion give?
- Opinion A: _____
- Opinion B: _____

4 Create one more supporting idea for each argument.
- Opinion A: _____
- Opinion B: _____

Skills for Debate

Read and learn how to organize your supporting arguments.

How Can You Organize Your Supporting Arguments?

The heart of any debate is the supporting arguments for each side. One of the keys to winning your debate is organizing your arguments effectively. The most common strategy is to organize your ideas in the **order of importance**. To do this, put your **strongest argument** first, your next strongest argument second, and so forth. Remember that a strong argument is one that you can support with **reasons** and **examples**. Effective arguments also have strong **social implications** or make strong **emotional appeals**. You must keep these factors in mind when you create your supporting arguments.

Practicing Debate Skills

Read the debate topic below and its arguments. Create reasons and examples for each argument. Then, place each of the arguments in order from most important to least important. Finally, explain why you placed the arguments in that order.

- **Debate Topic:** Countries should focus on economic development in the present and stress environmental problems in the future.

- **Arguments:** ⓐ It will be easier to help the environment in the future with better technology.

    Reasons: _____

    Example: _____
    _____

  ⓑ The current environmental problems we face are not that serious.

    Reasons: _____

    Example: _____
    _____

  ⓒ Economic development directly improves people's quality of life.

    Reasons: _____

    Example: _____
    _____

- **Order:** (   ) → (   ) → (   ) → (   )
- **Explanation:** _____
_____

Unit 01 B Debating the Topic

Creating Your Debate

Motion: Mass tourism should be restricted in order to protect nature.

What are your arguments? Get into two groups and plan for the debate. Decide whether your team is FOR (agree) or AGAINST (disagree) the motion. Then, create your ARE: Argument, Reason, and Example. Use the example arguments below and the research from your workbook to help create your arguments.

■ Example Arguments

FOR

Argument

Building amenities for tourists causes great harm to fragile ecosystems.

Reason

Some of the most popular tourist areas are located in areas that can be easily damaged by development, such as forests and beaches. Such construction can permanently alter the natural environment in these areas. The only way to protect these ecosystems is to outlaw mass tourism.

Example

For instance, the mining of coral for use in tourist hotels in the Philippines has destroyed many large coral reefs in the region.

AGAINST

Argument

Implementing a ban on tourism would be difficult to achieve.

Reason

As of today, around one billion people travel to foreign countries each year. It would be extremely difficult for authorities in any nation to monitor whether foreign visitors are coming for tourism or for other purposes. This would be a major drain on a government's resources.

Example

It would also be difficult to guarantee that somebody traveling abroad on business does not do any sightseeing. Simply allowing tourism is far more practical.

Arguments FOR/AGAINST the Motion

ARGUMENT 1

Argument

_____
_____
_____
_____
_____
_____

Reason

_____
_____
_____
_____
_____
_____

Example

_____
_____
_____
_____
_____
_____

ARGUMENT 2

Argument

_____
_____
_____
_____
_____
_____

Reason

_____
_____
_____
_____
_____
_____

Example

_____
_____
_____
_____
_____
_____

ARGUMENT 3

Argument

_____
_____
_____
_____
_____
_____

Reason

_____
_____
_____
_____
_____
_____

Example

_____
_____
_____
_____
_____
_____

Actual Debate

Now, it's time to debate. Use the flow chart below to help you organize the debate.
The introductory expressions have been provided to help you. Put your arguments in logical order and make clear rebuttals to the opposing team's arguments.

Agree Opening Statement
Our team is convinced that _____.

Agree Argument 1
The first reason we believe this is _____.

Rebuttal 1
The problem with your argument is _____.

Agree Argument 2
Secondly, _____.

Rebuttal 2
Despite your contention that _____, we hold the idea that _____.

Agree Argument 3
As for our third point, it is _____.

Agree Closing Statement
In spite of our opponent's arguments, it is obvious that _____.

Disagree Opening Statement
We feel the exact opposite. It is our belief that _____.

Rebuttal 1
You are mistaken to think that _____. A superior alternative would be to _____.

Disagree Argument 1
The argument we will make first is _____.

Rebuttal 2
Your argument is just not true. Rather, _____.

Disagree Argument 2
To continue, let us point out that _____.

Rebuttal 3
It is wrong to say that _____ since _____.

Disagree Argument 3
Our concluding argument is _____.

Disagree Closing Statement
Overall, we firmly believe that _____.

Sum Up the Debate

Finish the debate summary.

AGREEING SIDE'S ARGUMENT

The issue we debated today was _____.

The agree team argued that _____.

For starters, the pro team stated that _____.

Their example was _____
_____.

The second point they mentioned was _____.

For instance, _____
_____.

As for their third argument, it was _____.

In detail, they stated that _____
_____.

DISAGREEING SIDE'S ARGUMENT

Conversely, the opposing team felt that _____
_____.

Their first argument was that _____.

The evidence that they presented was _____
_____.

The team's second point was _____.

For example, _____
_____.

Their final assertion was that _____.

The support that they offered was _____
_____.

Unit 02 Privatizing Education

A. Discuss the following questions as a class.

1. What do you see in the picture above?
2. What subject are the students learning? Does it look challenging enough for their age?
3. Do you think that this is a public school or a private school? Explain your reasoning.

B. Answer the following questions with a partner.

1. Do you go to a public school or a private school?
2. What are some advantages of attending a private school?
3. What are some drawbacks of attending a private school?

Unit 02 A Learning about the Topic

Should all formal education be made private?

Read the passage and underline the main ideas.   Track 04

In nearly every measurable way, private schools offer a superior education to public schools. Students at private schools are far less likely to have behavioral problems and generally have much higher standardized test scores. With all of the benefits offered by private education, a number of parents have started to demand that public schools become privatized. Many persuasive arguments support such a change.

The main advantage of private schools is the superior education that they offer. Teachers at private schools are generally better prepared and more effective educators than public school instructors. This enables students at private schools to learn more and to get higher test scores. For instance, the average SAT score of private school students is almost 200 points higher than the average score of public school students. Likewise, private school teachers are **accountable** for their teaching. One of the main problems with public schools is that ineffective teachers rarely lose their jobs. Conversely, private school teachers must instruct students well. If they do not, then they can be fired. It must also be pointed out that private schools often have superior curricula. Unlike public schools, private schools can use a variety of teaching methods that make learning more **engaging** for students. A good example is Montessori schools, which teach students through projects and creative lessons.

While private schools offer many benefits, they are not perfect. One drawback is that private schools are hard to regulate. Since education at private schools is not standardized, it is difficult to guarantee that all students learn enough material. Another point to consider is that some private schools **swindle** parents and students. Some private school owners are **unscrupulous** and care more about making a profit than providing a quality education. These schools overcharge students. They may hire inexperienced teachers or use outdated, ineffective teaching methods. Students would suffer by receiving an inferior education while parents would waste thousands of dollars a year as their children are poorly educated. Finally, many parents cannot afford to pay for private schools. Private schools in the United States cost $8,500 per year on average for each student. Students from low-income homes would end up attending cheaper, inferior schools. This would **exacerbate** the education gap between rich and poor families.

Vocabulary Check

Choose the correct word for each definition.

| accountable | engaging | swindle | unscrupulous | exacerbate |

1 to cheat someone out of money

2 to make a situation worse or more severe

3 pleasing in a way that holds one's attention

4 being responsible for something

5 not honest or fair

Comprehension Questions

Check the correct answer for each question.

1 What evidence proves that students at private schools learn more?
- ☐ The fact that their teachers are better prepared and more effective educators
- ☐ The fact that their SAT scores are 200 points higher than public school students' scores

2 How does being able to fire teachers lead to a superior quality of education?
- ☐ It guarantees that teachers will follow the same specific teaching curriculum.
- ☐ It allows schools to get rid of teachers who do not instruct students effectively.

3 Why is it difficult to regulate the academic content taught by private schools?
- ☐ Because the curriculum is different at each private school
- ☐ Because the students at private schools do not learn enough material

4 How would the privatization of education widen the education gap between wealthy and impoverished families?
- ☐ It would force parents with low incomes to spend too much money on educating their children.
- ☐ It would lead to students from poorer families going to lower-quality schools.

Questions for Debate

Think of and share ideas to explore the debatable issues in the article. Be sure to state your opinion clearly and to provide one supporting idea for each opinion.

1 Do you attend a public school or a private school? What is the learning environment like?

   My school is _____

   _____.

   The learning environment there is _____

   _____.

2 What characteristics do you think are important for providing a high-quality education?

   Some of the most important characteristics are _____

   _____.

   These are important because _____

   _____.

3 Do you think that it is necessary for schools to be able to fire their teachers? Why or why not?

   To me, it seems that _____

   _____.

   The reason I say this is that _____

   _____.

4 What are some reasons that private schools can actually be worse than public schools?

   Some of the reasons are _____

   _____.

   For instance, _____

   _____.

5 Should the government regulate private schools as it does public schools? Explain.

   My feeling about this is _____

   _____.

   This is due to the fact that _____

   _____.

Opinion Examples

Look at the opinion examples about the motion below and answer the questions.

Motion: Public education should be replaced with private education.

Opinion A Track 05

Replacing public schools with private ones sounds plausible, but it will not work in practice. The primary obstacle is that private schools are too expensive. Sending just one child to a private school for a year costs $8,500 or more. For many parents—especially those with more than one child—this would be a huge financial burden. Even if cheaper private schools open, there is no guarantee that they will offer a better learning experience than public schools. Many private schools exist only so the owners can make a profit. They do not care if their students learn anything. The privatization of all education will surely lead to the opening of thousands of schools where students learn almost nothing.

Opinion B Track 06

It is a well-known fact that the government does not work efficiently. Therefore, it makes no sense for us to let the government educate our children. Private schools are far superior. One reason is that private schools have higher-quality teachers. Some public school teachers are good, but many are not. However, private school teachers must work hard, or else they will be fired. It is also necessary to keep in mind that students can learn more at private schools. While public schools are forced to follow a government-mandated curriculum, private schools have the freedom to teach students however they like. In most cases, this means giving students creative projects that help them develop their reasoning skills.

1 Underline the main idea of each opinion.

2 Which opinion is for the topic? Which one is against it?
   - FOR: _____
   - AGAINST: _____

3 What supporting ideas does each opinion give?
   - Opinion A: _____
   - Opinion B: _____

4 Create one more supporting idea for each argument.
   - Opinion A: _____
   - Opinion B: _____

Skills for Debate

Read and learn how to organize your supporting arguments.

How Can You Organize Your Supporting Arguments?

Along with organizing your arguments by their importance, you can also choose to have your ideas **develop sequentially**. This means introducing your **broadest argument** first and having your second and third arguments **elaborate on your first point**. To do this, simply decide which of your arguments is the most general and place it first. Then, put your more specific arguments afterward. Organizing your arguments this way **clarifies the main issue** and **highlights specific points** of your argument.

Practicing Debate Skills

Read the debate topics below. The first supporting argument for each side has been given for you. Come up with two more supporting arguments that build upon the first supporting argument.

1 All citizens should be required to graduate from college.

FOR
- Making sure that everyone is college educated will improve society.
- _____
- _____

AGAINST
- Not everybody has the ability or desire to attend college.
- _____
- _____

2 The government should invest more money into schools.

FOR
- Increased government spending will lead to a higher-quality education.
- _____
- _____

AGAINST
- Many governments already have too many expenses as it is.
- _____
- _____

Unit 02 B Debating the Topic

Creating Your Debate

Motion: Public education should be replaced with private education.

What are your arguments? Get into two groups and plan for the debate. Decide whether your team is FOR (agree) or AGAINST (disagree) the motion. Then, create your ARE: Argument, Reason, and Example. Use the example arguments below and the research from your workbook to help create your arguments.

■ Example Arguments

FOR	AGAINST
Argument	**Argument**
Students will be educated by more qualified and talented teachers at private schools.	The quality of education at private schools is not always better than at public schools.
Reason	**Reason**
Unlike public school teachers, private school teachers are held accountable for their instruction. Teachers must work hard to make sure that their students learn well. If they do not, then they are likely to lose their jobs. The students benefit by having teachers who work hard.	Some private schools outperform public schools, but a number of them do not. Poor-quality private schools may hire less experienced teachers, or they may give their teachers little feedback. This means that students do not always learn more at private schools.
Example	**Example**
In the United States, around 10 percent of private school teachers lose their jobs every year due to poor performance. In contrast, the firing rate for public school teachers is less than 1 percent.	On the PISA test given to 15-year-old students in the United States, the average test scores of private school students were only about 10 points higher than the scores of students in public schools. This is not a significant difference.

■ Arguments FOR/AGAINST the Motion

ARGUMENT 1

Argument

_____
_____
_____
_____
_____
_____

Reason

_____
_____
_____
_____
_____

Example

_____
_____
_____
_____
_____

ARGUMENT 2

Argument

_____
_____
_____
_____
_____
_____

Reason

_____
_____
_____
_____
_____

Example

_____
_____
_____
_____
_____

ARGUMENT 3

Argument

_____
_____
_____
_____
_____
_____

Reason

_____
_____
_____
_____
_____

Example

_____
_____
_____
_____
_____

Actual Debate

Now, it's time to debate. Use the flow chart below to help you organize the debate.
The introductory expressions have been provided to help you. Put your arguments in logical order and make clear rebuttals to the opposing team's arguments.

Agree Opening Statement
It is our team's firm conviction that _____.

Agree Argument 1
The most obvious point in our favor is that _____.

Rebuttal 1
The main flaw with the argument that _____ is that _____.

Agree Argument 2
In addition, we feel that _____.

Rebuttal 2
Your argument is false since _____.

Agree Argument 3
To conclude, we must bring up the point that _____.

Agree Closing Statement
Our team maintains the idea that _____.

Disagree Opening Statement
As for our side, we contend that _____.

Rebuttal 1
You wrongly assume that _____. Rather, consider that _____.

Disagree Argument 1
For starters, we believe that _____.

Rebuttal 2
Your belief that _____ is flawed because _____.

Disagree Argument 2
The next point we will make is that _____.

Rebuttal 3
You said that _____. Nevertheless, we believe that _____.

Disagree Argument 3
Finally, it is obvious that _____.

Disagree Closing Statement
In summary, we contend that _____.

Sum Up the Debate

Finish the debate summary.

AGREEING SIDE'S ARGUMENT

The topic of today's debate was _____.

The opinion of the first team was _____.

First, they claimed that _____.

In detail, they stated that _____
_____.

The next point that they mentioned was _____.

For instance, _____
_____.

Their final argument was _____.

More specifically, they claimed that _____
_____.

DISAGREEING SIDE'S ARGUMENT

The other team felt just the opposite and stated that _____
_____.

For one, it was their belief that _____.

Their supporting idea was _____
_____.

They also argued that _____.

In particular, they outlined that _____
_____.

As for their closing argument, it was _____.

The evidence that they offered was _____
_____.

Chapter 2

Developing Logical Supporting Reasons

Unit 03 Talking on Cell Phones on Public Transportation

Unit 04 Banning Bottled Water

Unit 03
Talking on Cell Phones on Public Transportation

A. Discuss the following questions as a class.
1. What do you see in the picture above?
2. What might the woman's conversation be about?
3. Do you think the other passengers on the train are irritated by the woman's conversation?

B. Answer the following questions with a partner.
1. Do you ever make phone calls when you are on public transportation? Why or why not?
2. Why would it be inappropriate for people to talk on their phones while taking public transportation?
3. What are some ways that people can use their phones without irritating other passengers?

Unit 03   A   Learning about the Topic

Should people not be allowed to talk on their cell phones on public transportation?

Read the passage and underline the main ideas.   Track 07

Subway passengers in Japan who want to talk on their phones are in for a big surprise. Talking on cell phones on public transportation is forbidden in Japan. This is a **denial** of people's personal freedom, but there is a good reason for it. Having phone conversations on public transportation is an **inconsiderate** activity that makes other people uncomfortable, so it must be prohibited.

Primarily, talking on the phone is rude. In enclosed spaces such as buses and subways, other passengers are forced to listen to people's phone conversations. Hearing these conversations is intrusive and can annoy other people. A recent poll by the Associated Press found that 78 percent of Americans oppose talking on the phone during airplane flights because it is **irritating**. The second reason to ban talking on phones is that people are more likely to have inappropriate conversations in public. When people talk with their friends while taking public transportation together, they are more likely to be aware of what they talk about. This is not the case with cell phones. People who talk on cell phones often forget that other people can hear their conversations. Thus, they are more likely to discuss personal topics that other passengers do not want to hear. Third, most features of phones today do not require speaking anyway. Rather than making phone calls, people can surf the Internet, send text messages, and play games in near silence.

A number of people insist that they should have the right to use their cell phones on public transportation. For one, a ban on cell phone conversations is an **excessive** restriction of personal freedom. It is lawful for individuals to do whatever they please so long as they do not directly harm other people. Talking on cell phones while taking public transportation is inconsiderate, but it does not hurt others. Additionally, cell phones were designed to be used in public places. When people are riding public transportation, it is logical for them to want to use their time efficiently by contacting other people. For instance, people often use their cell phones to **confirm** meeting times and locations with friends. Finally, other passengers can choose to move to another seat or train car if they are annoyed by a nearby phone conversation. They can also listen to music or play games on their own cell phones to block out the sound of the other person's talking.

Vocabulary Check

Choose the correct word for each definition.

> denial   inconsiderate   irritating   excessive   confirm

1 to check and make sure of something
2 the act of not allowing someone to have something
3 not thinking about the rights and feelings of others
4 going beyond what is usual or necessary
5 causing someone to feel annoyed or angry

Comprehension Questions

Check the correct answer for each question.

1 What is true about taking the subway in Japan?

  ☐ Passengers cannot use their cell phones in any way.
  ☐ Riders are not allowed to talk on their cell phones.

2 Why does talking on a cell phone make people more likely to have inappropriate conversations in public?

  ☐ Because they are less likely to be aware that they are in a public place
  ☐ Because they usually have conversations with their friends

3 How can people use cell phones in a way that does not irritate other people?

  ☐ They can make phone calls while using their headphones.
  ☐ They can play games or surf the Internet almost silently.

4 In what way is disallowing people to talk on their cell phones an excessive control of personal freedoms?

  ☐ Because cell phones were designed to be used in public places
  ☐ Because talking on cell phones does not directly hurt other people

Questions for Debate

Think of and share ideas to explore the debatable issues in the article. Be sure to state your opinion clearly and to provide one supporting idea for each opinion.

1. Do you ever talk on your cell phone while riding on public transportation? Why or why not?

   When I take public transportation, I _____.

   I do this because _____.

2. Why would cities make it illegal to talk on cell phones while riding on public transportation?

   My opinion about this is _____.

   To go into detail, _____.

3. If having phone conversations on public transportation were made illegal, should it also be illegal for people to have conversations with other passengers? Explain.

   To me, it seems that _____.

   In particular, _____.

4. What is an appropriate way for passengers to respond when somebody talks on their cell phone?

   I contend that _____.

   My reasons for feeling this way are _____.

5. Rather than banning cell phone conversations, how else could governments solve this problem?

   A better possible solution may be _____.

   I think this will be more effective because _____.

Opinion Examples

Look at the opinion examples about the motion below and answer the questions.

Motion: People should not be allowed to talk on their cell phones on public transportation.

Opinion A Track 08

To me, it makes perfect sense to ban people from talking on their cell phones on public transportation. For one, public transportation consists of enclosed spaces. If we meet somebody on the street talking on his or her phone, we can walk away from that person easily. But on public transportation, people are forced to listen to other people's conversations. Furthermore, when people ride on public transportation, they are often tired or stressed out. They are usually commuting to or from work or school or have been shopping, so they probably want a chance to rest. If people talk on their phones, then other passengers will get more anxiety.

Opinion B Track 09

I find it shocking that people actually want to make it illegal to talk on cell phones on public transportation. I think this is a ridiculous idea for many reasons. First, there is nothing illegal about having a conversation in public. Some other passengers may not like it, but talking does not harm other people. Therefore, there is no precedent to make phone conversations illegal. Banning people from calling on thier cell phones on public transportation would also be hugely inconvenient. The purpose of cell phones is to allow people to contact others when they are out. Making it illegal to talk on phones would prevent people from arranging meetings or multitasking with their work.

1. Underline the main idea of each opinion.

2. Which opinion is for the topic? Which one is against it?
   - FOR: _____
   - AGAINST: _____

3. What supporting ideas does each opinion give?
   - Opinion A: _____
   - Opinion B: _____

4. Create one more supporting idea for each argument.
   - Opinion A: _____
   - Opinion B: _____

Skills for Debate

Read and learn how to create logical supporting reasons.

How Can You Create Logical Supporting Reasons?

Supporting reasons develop your arguments to make them **more persuasive** and **easier to understand**. For each argument, you should make around two to five sentences of supporting reasons. The key aspect of supporting reasons is that they are **logical**. Logical reasons **explain the details** of your argument. These details allow you to **draw conclusions** about the validity of your assertion. To make your supporting reasons logical, you must be sure that they clearly develop your ideas.

Practicing Debate Skills

Read the following arguments and their supporting reasons. Give logical reasons to fill in the missing details. Finally, rewrite the conclusions to make them more logical.

1 Argument: Having loud phone conversations on public transportation is disrespectful to other passengers.

Details: When people are in public places, they should respect the feelings of other people. However, by talking loudly on their phones, they _____

_____

Conclusion: As a result, people will be more likely to talk on their phones at home.

Rewrite: As a result, _____

_____

2 Argument: People can still communicate on their phones without having to have spoken conversations.

Details: Today's smartphones have many features that make it possible to communicate without having to call other people. Some of these features include _____

_____

Conclusion: Therefore, it should be illegal for people to carry their cell phones on public transportation.

Rewrite: Therefore, _____

_____

Unit 03 B Debating the Topic

Creating Your Debate

Motion: People should not be allowed to talk on their cell phones on public transportation.

What are your arguments? Get into two groups and plan for the debate. Decide whether your team is FOR (agree) or AGAINST (disagree) the motion. Then, create your ARE: Argument, Reason, and Example. Use the example arguments below and the research from your workbook to help create your arguments.

■ **Example Arguments**

FOR

Argument

Having phone conversations on public transportation can irritate other passengers.

Reason

On public transportation, people are forced to stay in close contact with others. Because personal space is limited, it is easy for people to annoy other passengers by talking on their phones.

Example

For instance, 78 percent of Americans feel that talking on the phone during plane flights should be outlawed because the noise distracts other passengers.

AGAINST

Argument

A ban on phone conversations on public transportation is unlikely to work.

Reason

People would still want to talk on their phones even if doing so is banned. Rather than making it illegal to talk on phones, it would be better for cities to create designed places where people can and cannot talk on the phone.

Example

Some cities in Europe have created separate cars on subway trains where people are allowed to talk on their phones. At the same time, they have created phone-free cars where people are not permitted to use their phones.

Arguments FOR/AGAINST the Motion

ARGUMENT 1

Argument

Reason

Example

ARGUMENT 2

Argument

Reason

Example

ARGUMENT 3

Argument

Reason

Example

Actual Debate

Now, it's time to debate. Use the flow chart below to help you organize the debate.
The introductory expressions have been provided to help you. Put your arguments in logical order and make clear rebuttals to the opposing team's arguments.

Agree Opening Statement
To us, there is no doubt that _____.

Disagree Opening Statement
We completely disagree. Our stance is that _____.

Agree Argument 1
First of all, we contend that _____.

Rebuttal 1
Your argument is absolutely wrong because _____.

Disagree Argument 1
Our opening argument is that _____.

Rebuttal 1
Despite your belief that _____, it is our contention that _____.

Rebuttal 2
You falsely argue that _____.
The fact is _____.

Agree Argument 2
In addition, consider that _____.

Disagree Argument 2
Another point we must mention is _____.

Rebuttal 2
The problem with your statement that _____ is the fact that _____.

Rebuttal 3
The argument that _____ is incorrect since _____.

Agree Argument 3
Lastly, _____.

Disagree Argument 3
As for our closing argument, _____.

Agree Closing Statement
In spite of our opponent's arguments, we feel that _____.

Disagree Closing Statement
To summarize, we believe that _____.

Sum Up the Debate

Finish the debate summary.

AGREEING SIDE'S ARGUMENT

The topic of today's debate was _____.

The main opinion of the first team was _____.

One argument that they gave was _____.

Their supporting detail was _____

_____.

In addition, they explained that _____

For instance, _____

_____.

The final point that they mentioned was _____.

Specifically, they stated that _____

_____.

DISAGREEING SIDE'S ARGUMENT

Conversely, the opposing team believed that _____

_____.

Their first argument was that _____.

The details that they talked about included _____

_____.

Second of all, _____.

Their supporting evidence was _____

_____.

The last point that they mentioned was _____.

They illustrated this by talking about _____

_____.

Unit 04 Banning Bottled Water

A. Discuss the following questions as a class.
1. What do you see in the picture above?
2. Why do you think that the boy is drinking bottled water?
3. What are some other ways that the boy could rehydrate besides drinking bottled water?

B. Answer the following questions with a partner.
1. How often do you drink bottled water?
2. What are some reasons that people prefer to drink bottled water over tap water?
3. How can producing bottled water be harmful for the environment?

Unit 04 A Learning about the Topic

Should people stop drinking bottled water?

Read the passage and underline the main ideas. Track 10

Since 1990, global consumption of bottled water has more than quadrupled. The number of bottles of water sold each year now exceeds 200 billion, with the United States alone consuming one-quarter of this amount. The popularity of bottled water is best explained by its supposed superior water quality and **portability**. As so many people enjoy drinking bottled water, it would seem that any attempt to ban it would surely fail.

People prefer to drink bottled water because the water quality is superior. The tap water in many nations is not safe to drink. Chemicals, garbage, and other forms of pollution make it **undrinkable**. In contrast, most bottled water comes from purer sources, such as mountain springs. Drinking bottled water lets people be sure that they are consuming fresh water free of **toxins**. In addition, though plastic water bottles can create lots of waste, they are also recyclable. The majority of plastic water bottles are made from polyethylene terephthalate, otherwise known as PET. This is a thin plastic designed to be recycled without difficulty. Plastic water bottles can be reused to make bags, carpets, and even jacket linings. The last point to mention is the convenience of bottled water. Plastic water bottles are light, easy to store, and easy to carry. This makes them the best way to rehydrate when you are on the go.

Not everybody is on the bottled water bandwagon, though. For one, there is little reason to believe that bottled water is higher quality than tap water. The soft drink companies Pepsi and Coca-Cola are also two of the biggest sellers of bottled water. Most of their bottled water is actually tap water. Next, even though it is possible to recycle plastic water bottles, an **insignificant** number of people actually do. Studies have shown that only 1 in 5 Americans recycle their water bottles. Even worse, making plastic bottles is a huge waste of energy resources. The production of plastic bottles worldwide uses 17 million oil barrels annually. This is enough to power 1 million cars for a year. Finally, plastic water bottles should be banned on the grounds of cost. A two-liter bottle of water costs $1.50. In contrast, two liters of tap water costs about $0.02. The tremendous cost of bottled water can put great financial **strain** on people with lower incomes who live in places where the tap water is unsafe to drink.

Vocabulary Check

Choose the correct word for each definition.

> portability   undrinkable   toxin   insignificant   strain

1 something that causes illness; a pollutant _____
2 the quality of being easy to transport and carry _____
3 something difficult to deal with that causes harm _____
4 unhealthy or unpleasant to drink _____
5 small or unimportant _____

Comprehension Questions

Check the correct answer for each question.

1 How many bottles of water do people in the United States drink annually?
- ☐ 50 billion
- ☐ 200 billion

2 Why is bottled water supposedly better to drink than tap water?
- ☐ Because it is produced by popular soft drink companies
- ☐ Because it uses water from fresh sources such as mountain springs

3 What is the advantage of using PET plastic to make water bottles?
- ☐ It is light and thin, so it is easy for people to carry.
- ☐ It can be easily recycled into many products.

4 How is the argument that water bottles are easy to recycle made invalid?
- ☐ By the fact that only 20 percent of U.S. citizens actually recycle their used water bottles
- ☐ By the fact that a two-liter bottle of water is 75 times more expensive than the same amount of tap water

Questions for Debate

Think of and share ideas to explore the debatable issues in the article. Be sure to state your opinion clearly and to provide one supporting idea for each opinion.

1. Do you or your family ever drink tap water instead of drinking bottled water? Why or why not?

   In my case, _____
   _____.

   This is due to the fact that _____
   _____.

2. Only about 20 percent of people recycle their water bottles. Is this an appropriate amount?

   I believe that _____
   _____.

   To be more specific, _____
   _____.

3. Do you think that most people would still drink bottled water even if they knew how much energy making the bottles requires? Explain.

   From my point of view, it is clear that _____
   _____.

   For example, _____
   _____.

4. Does the convenience that bottled water offers outweigh its environmental drawbacks?

   There is no doubt that _____
   _____.

   This is due to the fact that _____
   _____.

5. Instead of drinking bottled water, what are some other ways that people can stay hydrated when they are out?

   Some other ways to stay hydrated include _____
   _____.

   These are better alternatives because _____
   _____.

Opinion Examples

Look at the opinion examples about the motion below and answer the questions.

Motion: Companies should be allowed to continue to produce bottled water.

Opinion A Track 11

There is no doubt that bottled water should be banned. These plastic bottles may be designed to be recycled, but the truth is that only a fifth of them are. This means that billions of used water bottles are thrown into landfills each year and create land pollution that will be around for centuries. Not only do these bottles pollute the land, but they also pollute the air. What few people realize is that making plastic water bottles requires a huge amount of fuel. Each year, 17 million barrels of oil are burned to make plastic water bottles. This is a huge waste of energy and an unnecessary source of pollution.

Opinion B Track 12

I drink bottled water almost every day, and I don't see a problem with it. The main reason that I like bottled water is that it is usually cleaner. The tap water in my city is not safe to drink whereas most bottled water comes from clean sources that are free of pollution. To be sure that my water is safe, I always drink bottled water. Another reason that I prefer to drink water from bottles is that it is convenient. When I am out exercising or playing sports, I can easily carry bottled water in my bag. When I drink all of the water, I can throw away the bottle. I don't have to worry about carrying an empty bottle around with me until I get home.

1 Underline the main idea of each opinion.

2 Which opinion is for the topic? Which one is against it?

- FOR: _____

- AGAINST: _____

3 What supporting ideas does each opinion give?

- Opinion A: _____

- Opinion B: _____

4 Create one more supporting idea for each argument.

- Opinion A: _____

- Opinion B: _____

Skills for Debate

Read and learn how to create logical supporting reasons.

How Can You Create Logical Supporting Reasons?

A logical argument has a **clear premise** followed by a **reasonable conclusion**. When you make your arguments, you should try to avoid creating **logical fallacies**. These are arguments that contain errors in reasoning that weaken your argument. There are many logical fallacies, but some of the most common include:

1. **slippery slope** – arguing a conclusion that does not clearly relate to the premise
2. **ad hominem** – criticizing a person's character rather than his or her arguments
3. **straw man** – oversimplifying an opponent's argument and attacking that weak viewpoint

Practicing Debate Skills

Read the flowing logical supporting reasons. Decide which type of logical fallacy each reason is. Finally, rewrite the fallacy so that it is logically correct.

1. People who choose to drink bottled water hate the environment.
   - Fallacy Type: _____
   - Rewrite: _____

2. The people who want to ban bottled water are ignorant and do not understand the real world.
   - Fallacy Type: _____
   - Rewrite: _____

3. If we continue to allow people to drink bottled water, then it will definitely lead to the destruction of the planet.
   - Fallacy Type: _____
   - Rewrite: _____

Unit 04 B Debating the Topic

Creating Your Debate

Motion: Companies should be allowed to contiue to produce bottled water.

What are your arguments? Get into two groups and plan for the debate. Decide whether your team is FOR (agree) or AGAINST (disagree) the motion. Then, create your ARE: Argument, Reason, and Example. Use the example arguments below and the research from your workbook to help create your arguments.

■ **Example Arguments**

FOR	AGAINST
Argument	**Argument**
Bottled water provides a source of safe drinking water for millions of people.	The production of bottled water creates huge amounts of pollution.
Reason	**Reason**
In dozens of countries around the world, the water is not safe to drink. These countries have high levels of pollution or inadequate water treatment facilities. Bottled water offers an easy way for these people to drink pure, safe water.	Making the plastic bottles for water requires lots of energy and produces a great deal of pollution. None of this pollution would occur if people simply drank tap water.
Example	**Example**
The World Health Organization (WHO) recently reported that 780 million people worldwide do not have access to clean drinking water. The organization recommends that these people drink bottled water.	Producing one plastic water bottle requires three times the amount of water that the bottle actually holds. The total amount of oil used to produce all plastic water bottles exceeds 17 million barrels annually.

Arguments FOR/AGAINST the Motion

ARGUMENT 1

Argument

_____
_____
_____
_____
_____
_____
_____

Reason

_____
_____
_____
_____
_____
_____
_____

Example

_____
_____
_____
_____
_____
_____
_____

ARGUMENT 2

Argument

_____
_____
_____
_____
_____
_____
_____

Reason

_____
_____
_____
_____
_____
_____
_____

Example

_____
_____
_____
_____
_____
_____
_____

ARGUMENT 3

Argument

_____
_____
_____
_____
_____
_____
_____

Reason

_____
_____
_____
_____
_____
_____
_____

Example

_____
_____
_____
_____
_____
_____
_____

Actual Debate

Now, it's time to debate. Use the flow chart below to help you organize the debate.
The introductory expressions have been provided to help you. Put your arguments in logical order and make clear rebuttals to the opposing team's arguments.

Agree Opening Statement
It is our team's firm conviction that _____.

Disagree Opening Statement
On the contrary, it is our supposition that _____.

Agree Argument 1
For one, _____.

Rebuttal 1
The notion that _____ is erroneous since _____.

Disagree Argument 1
Our opening argument is _____.

Rebuttal 1
Your argument is flawed because _____.

Agree Argument 2
As for our next point, it is _____.

Rebuttal 2
The problem with your second point is _____.

Disagree Argument 2
In addition, we feel that _____.

Rebuttal 2
Our opponents wrongly contend that _____.

Agree Argument 3
The final point we will make is _____.

Rebuttal 3
Your belief that _____ is not true. Instead, _____.

Disagree Argument 3
Lastly, _____.

Agree Closing Statement
In summary, _____.

Disagree Closing Statement
Overall, we contend that _____.

Sum Up the Debate

Finish the debate summary.

AGREEING SIDE'S ARGUMENT

The topic that we dealt with today was _____.

It was the opinion of the first team that _____.

First, they claimed that _____.

Their supporting detail was _____
_____.

Next, they presented the notion that _____.

The example that they gave was _____
_____.

Finally, the agree side claimed that _____.

Their evidence was _____
_____.

DISAGREEING SIDE'S ARGUMENT

The other team argued the opposite by stating that _____
_____.

_____ was their first argument.

They pointed out that _____
_____ to bolster their argument.

Their second point was _____.

To go into detail, _____
_____.

Their closing argument was _____.

For instance, _____
_____.

Chapter 3

Developing Effective Supporting Reasons

Unit 05 Returning Art Stolen during Wars

Unit 06 Single-Gender Schools

Unit 05 Returning Art Stolen during Wars

WARM-UP

A. Discuss the following questions as a class.

1. What do you see in the picture above?
2. What country do you think that these sculptures originally came from?
3. Where do you think these pieces are being displayed?

B. Answer the following questions with a partner.

1. Do you think that a piece of artwork belongs in the country where it was made?
2. Is it right for nations to steal valuables from the nations that they defeat in war?
3. Should countries be expected to return stolen artwork if they take good care of the pieces?

Unit 05 A Learning about the Topic

Should artwork stolen during wars be returned to its home countries?

Read the passage and underline the main ideas. Track 13

In 2013, a collection of 1,500 pieces of artwork valued at 1.5 billion dollars was discovered. The works were **seized** by the Nazis before and during World War II. However, the Germans were hardly the first to steal artwork from other nations in times of war. Armies throughout history have looted artwork, jewelry, and other treasures from other countries as a reward for their battle victories. Despite this, is it right for nations to keep artwork that they have plundered from their opponents?

On the one hand, several members of the international community strongly believe that stolen artwork should be returned. The Hague Convention for the Protection of Cultural Property explicitly bans the looting of artwork during wartime. The **basis** for this is that a nation's artwork serves as a foundation for its cultural heritage. Moreover, while there are some instances of looted artwork not having a clear owner, this is not true of all artwork. The majority of stolen works have owners in the form of national governments and heirs. These pieces should be returned to their rightful owners. For example, in 2005, Japan returned a **monument** to South Korea since it clearly belonged to the nation. Third, the nations that request the return of plundered works are usually capable of preserving them. When stable and wealthy nations such as China and South Korea demand the return of looted pieces, their requests should be honored.

On the other hand, looting by **victorious** armies has long been a common practice. Countries fought wars with the intention of stealing treasures from enemy nations. This allowed them to finance their wars and to compensate their soldiers. Thus, victorious nations should be given the right to hold on to the pieces that they have lawfully obtained. Moreover, returning most looted artwork would be nearly impossible. Much stolen artwork was produced by artists who died long ago. These include some works of Pablo Picasso that were looted by the Germans. In some cases, entire **civilizations** that produced the stolen artifacts no longer exist, such as the Aztecs from Central America. Finally, looted pieces could be ruined if they are returned to their home nations. For instance, Egypt has demanded the return of its plundered artworks. However, the country now faces many social and governmental problems, so there is a high possibility that returned pieces would be lost or destroyed.

Vocabulary Check

Choose the correct word for each definition.

| seize | basis | monument | victorious | civilization |

1 to take something in a forceful and sudden way　　　　_____
2 a building or statue that honors a person or event　　　_____
3 something from which another thing can develop　　　　_____
4 a particular developed and well-organized society　　　 _____
5 having won a battle or competition　　　　　　　　　　 _____

Comprehension Questions

Check the correct answer for each question.

1 What was outlined by the Hague Convention?
   ☐ That all stolen artwork should be given back to its original owners
   ☐ That armies are not allowed to steal artwork from other countries during wars

2 Why should looted artwork be returned to stable and wealthy nations?
   ☐ Because these nations are able to take care of the works properly
   ☐ Because these nations have lost more artwork than unstable and poor nations

3 For what reason did nations originally steal valuable artwork from the nations that they defeated?
   ☐ They did it in order to cover their war expenses and to pay their soldiers' salaries.
   ☐ They wanted to steal works of art that were produced by artists who died long ago.

4 What would probably happen if artwork stolen from Egypt is returned to the country?
   ☐ The returned pieces would probably be well preserved.
   ☐ The artwork would likely disappear or be destroyed.

Questions for Debate

Think of and share ideas to explore the debatable issues in the article. Be sure to state your opinion clearly and to provide one supporting idea for each opinion.

1 Has your country ever stolen artwork from other nations, or have other nations stolen artwork from your country? How does this make you feel?

   To the best of my knowledge, my country has _____
   _____.

   The way that I feel about this is _____
   _____.

2 Should countries be allowed to keep works of art that have no clear owner?

   It is my opinion that _____
   _____.

   The reason I believe this is _____
   _____.

3 How would keeping looted artwork affect a country's relationships with other nations?

   As far as I am concerned, _____
   _____.

   For instance, _____
   _____.

4 Should a nation's economic or political situation be considered when it requests the return of looted artwork?

   The most logical thing to do in this case is _____
   _____.

   To give you a better idea, think about how _____
   _____.

5 Aside from returning stolen artwork, what else can nations do to compensate the countries they have stolen artwork from?

   It is my conviction that _____
   _____.

   More specifically, _____
   _____.

Opinion Examples

Look at the opinion examples about the motion below and answer the questions.

Motion: Artwork stolen during wartime should be returned to its home countries.

Opinion A Track 14

It is unrealistic to expect nations to return artwork that they have rightfully taken. To begin with, most of the artwork that has been looted was taken at a time when it was acceptable to do so. Until the 20th century, nearly all wars were funded by stolen artwork. We cannot punish nations for their past actions now, especially because they were acceptable at the time. In any event, much of the plundered artwork is well preserved. The pieces are proudly on display in museums throughout the world. Millions of people can see and appreciate these works as they are. If they are returned to their home nations, the works could be lost forever. Is that really a better alternative?

Opinion B Track 15

Stealing is never the right thing to do. This is why plundered artwork must be returned immediately. For one, our society strictly bans armies from looting other nations. While stealing artwork may have been acceptable in the past, today it is not. Therefore, these stolen works should be given back to their home nations as soon as possible. Another point to consider is that these plundered pieces form the national culture of their home nations. Important works are fundamental parts of a country's history. Pieces such as the Silver Bible belonging to the Czech Republic must stay in their home nations so that their people can better understand the heritage of their home countries.

1 Underline the main idea of each opinion.

2 Which opinion is for the topic? Which one is against it?
- FOR: _____
- AGAINST: _____

3 What supporting ideas does each opinion give?
- Opinion A: _____
- Opinion B: _____

4 Create one more supporting idea for each argument.
- Opinion A: _____
- Opinion B: _____

Skills for Debate

Read and learn how to create effective supporting reasons.

How Can You Create Effective Supporting Reasons?

In addition to being logical, your supporting reasons must be **effective**. An effective supporting reason provides **details** and **justification** for your argument. To ensure that your reasons are logical, keep the following three points in mind. First, answer **what** your argument means. Describe relevant details for your argument by outlining the actions that can occur because of it. The second step is to describe **why** you are making your argument. Connect your argument clearly with your team's overall stance. Lastly, mention **how** your argument will affect society in either a good or a bad way. Addressing these questions will make your arguments clear and effective.

Practicing Debate Skills

Read the arguments below. Create supporting reasons for each argument. Make sure that your ideas show logical progression. Some words have been provided to help you.

1 Taking art classes at school helps children develop their creativity.

- **what:** When children study art at school, they can _____

- **why:** This is important for the development of their creativity because _____

- **how:** Consequently, having students take art classes will lead them to _____

2 The government should censor artwork to prevent the spread of harmful ideas.

- **what:** Artwork can sometimes depict images that are _____

- **why:** The reason that this presents such a major issue is _____

- **how:** By censoring artwork, the government can _____

Unit 05 B Debating the Topic

Creating Your Debate

Motion: Artwork stolen during wartime should be returned to its home countries.

What are your arguments? Get into two groups and plan for the debate. Decide whether your team is FOR (agree) or AGAINST (disagree) the motion. Then, create your ARE: Argument, Reason, and Example. Use the example arguments below and the research from your workbook to help create your arguments.

■ Example Arguments

FOR

Argument

Plundered artwork should be returned because it belongs to the nations that originally produced it.

Reason

Looted artwork was stolen from the nations that lost wars. The losing nations did not give permission to have their works taken by other countries. Since stealing is wrong, it is similarly wrong for nations to keep artwork that they have plundered.

Example

The international community specifically banned the looting of artwork during wartimes with the adoption of the Hague Convention for the Protection of Cultural Property.

AGAINST

Argument

The looting of artwork is a natural consequence of war.

Reason

During war, nations always suffer losses. Their soldiers die on the battlefield, and their citizens have their homes destroyed. It is only natural to expect victorious armies to loot valuable works of art from losing nations.

Example

There is a common saying: "To the victor go the spoils." This refers to the idea of victorious nations taking items of value from the countries that they defeat in war.

Arguments FOR/AGAINST the Motion

ARGUMENT 1

Argument

Reason

Example

ARGUMENT 2

Argument

Reason

Example

ARGUMENT 3

Argument

Reason

Example

Actual Debate

Now, it's time to debate. Use the flow chart below to help you organize the debate.
The introductory expressions have been provided to help you. Put your arguments in logical order and make clear rebuttals to the opposing team's arguments.

Agree Opening Statement
The main position held by our team is _____.

Disagree Opening Statement
Unlike our opponents, we are convinced that _____.

Agree Argument 1
To start off with, _____.

Rebuttal 1
The main drawback to your point is _____.

Disagree Argument 1
As for our first point, it is _____.

Rebuttal 1
We disagree with your point. Consider that _____.

Rebuttal 2
It is incorrect to assume that _____ since _____.

Agree Argument 2
Next, let us point out that _____.

Disagree Argument 2
Additionally, _____.

Rebuttal 2
You still have it wrong. The fact is that _____.

Rebuttal 3
Despite your contention that _____, we feel that _____.

Agree Argument 3
We will conclude by mentioning that _____.

Disagree Argument 3
Our last argument is _____.

Agree Closing Statement
Our overall stance remains that _____.

Disagree Closing Statement
To summarize, we still maintain that _____.

Sum Up the Debate

Finish the debate summary.

AGREEING SIDE'S ARGUMENT

The motion that we focused on today was _____.

On the one hand, the members of the pro side argued that _____.

First of all, _____.

The evidence that they offered was _____

_____.

The next point that they made was _____.

In detail, they posited that _____

_____.

Their concluding argument was _____

_____

_____ was their supporting reasoning.

DISAGREEING SIDE'S ARGUMENT

On the contrary, the other team firmly believed that _____

_____.

Their opening argument was _____.

To go into detail, _____

_____.

Their second point was that _____.

For example, _____

_____.

They wrapped up by pointing out that _____.

The proof that they offered was _____

_____.

Unit 06
Single-Gender Schools

A. Discuss the following questions as a class.

1. What do you see in the picture above?
2. Do you think that the students in the picture are concentrating on their work? Explain.
3. How does attending school with students of both genders affect the learning environment?

B. Answer the following questions with a partner.

1. Do you attend a single-sex school or a coeducational school?
2. Would attending a single-gender school affect students' ability to study?
3. Do you believe that teachers treat students differently at single-sex schools? Why or why not?

Unit 06 A Learning about the Topic

Should all schools be single gender only?

Read the passage and underline the main ideas.  Track 16

Single-sex schools were the norm until the 19th century. From then onward, coeducational schools became common. Today, only Singapore, the United Kingdom, South Korea, and a few other nations have a significant number of single-sex schools. These nations may have the right idea. A growing body of research **indicates** that single-sex schools offer superior learning environments to coeducational schools.

A great advantage of single-sex schools is that they can better meet the unique educational needs of boys and girls. Boys learn best through classroom activities whereas girls perform better by having class discussions. Separating students based on sex can enable schools to teach them according to their academic needs. This is partially due to the next point: Having boys and girls go to school together creates distractions from learning. Boys and girls in elementary school may fight or bully each other. Older students may feel physical **attraction** toward one another. These interactions make it difficult for students to focus on their studies. A final upside to single-sex schools is that all of the students can receive an **equivalent** amount of attention. At coeducational schools, teachers often pay more attention to boys than they do to girls. Multiple studies, including ones by the journal *Childhood Education*, have shown that teachers are far more likely to call on male students and to ignore female students.

However, single-sex schools have some drawbacks. Chiefly, they do not prepare students for the real world. As adults, people have to get along with members of the opposite sex all the time. Going to a coeducational school enables children to learn about and understand the differences between the sexes, and this is an important lesson for succeeding in life. Another point is the long-term emotional issues created by single-sex schools. Boys suffer greatly by attending boys-only schools. Research by the Institution of Education in London found that men who went to boys' schools are more likely to suffer from **depression** or to get divorced as adults. These men were unable to develop an understanding of the emotional needs of girls since they rarely interacted with them as children. Many also oppose single-sex schools since they are a symbol of the male-dominated societies of the past. The main reason that schools were separated by gender until the 19th century was that girls did not attend school. In this way, gender-segregated schools **reinforce** the idea that girls do not deserve the same education as boys.

Vocabulary Check

Choose the correct word for each definition.

| indicate | attraction | equivalent | depression | reinforce |

1 to give support to an idea or a behavior _____
2 to show or suggest that something is true _____
3 being the same in amount or number _____
4 the feeling that makes someone attracted to another person _____
5 a state of feeling very sad _____

Comprehension Questions

Check the correct answer for each question.

1 Which of the following assignments would be better suited to a girls-only class? Choose TWO correct answers.

☐ Summarizing a short story read in class   ☐ Creating sentences from new vocabulary words
☐ Putting together a puzzle   ☐ Making a graph about students' favorite foods

2 How are boys and girls treated differently by teachers in coeducational schools?

☐ Teachers usually give male students higher grades than they give female students.
☐ Teachers are more likely to respond to male students and not to listen to female students.

3 Why do coeducational schools help students prepare for the adult world?

☐ They teach children how to relate to the opposite sex.
☐ They teach children important lessons for succeeding in life.

4 For what reason are men who attended boys' schools more likely to get divorced?

☐ Because they believe that girls do not deserve the same education as boys
☐ Because they do not properly understand the emotional needs of girls

Questions for Debate

Think of and share ideas to explore the debatable issues in the article. Be sure to state your opinion clearly and to provide one supporting idea for each opinion.

1 Would you prefer to attend a coeducational school or a single-sex school? Why?

In my case, I would rather _____
_____.

I feel this way because _____
_____.

2 What are some differences between boys and girls in terms of their personalities and interests?

Boys and girls are different in terms of _____
_____.

More specifically, _____
_____.

3 Why do you think that teachers often pay more attention to male students than to female students?

The reason this probably happens is that _____
_____.

For example, _____
_____.

4 How do coeducational schools better help students to prepare for the adult world?

The advantage of coeducational schools is _____
_____.

The importance of this is _____
_____.

5 Instead of making gender-segregated schools, what could an alternative for teaching boys and girls more effectively be?

A superior alternative might be _____
_____.

This would work better because _____
_____.

Opinion Examples

Look at the opinion examples about the motion below and answer the questions.

Motion: It is better for students to attend single-sex schools.

Opinion A Track 17

The world is not single-sex, and our schools shouldn't be either. The main problem with single-sex schools is that they don't teach students how to befriend members of the other sex. Boys and girls have different emotional and social needs, and it is important for children to be aware of these differences. As adults, they will have to interact with members of the other sex regularly. In addition, single-sex schools can cause children to develop gender stereotypes. Girls may believe that all boys enjoy sports and physical activities. Boys may think that all girls are emotional and artistic. When boys and girls are exposed to one another, they can learn about each other and embrace their differences.

Opinion B Track 18

Ever since my first year of middle school, I have only attended girls' schools. Overall, it has been a great experience. One reason is that single-sex schools are more comfortable. My friends who go to coed schools always talk about how mean the boy students can be. They say that they are embarrassed to participate in class because the boys make fun of them. But at my girls' school, all of the students respect everybody and their opinions. I also like my girls-only school because of the lessons. At my school, we have a lot of classes that are suited for girls. We have many reading, writing, and art classes. Even the math and science classes are designed to help girls learn better.

1 Underline the main idea of each opinion.

2 Which opinion is for the topic? Which one is against it?
- FOR: _____
- AGAINST: _____

3 What supporting ideas does each opinion give?
- Opinion A: _____
- Opinion B: _____

4 Create one more supporting idea for each argument.
- Opinion A: _____
- Opinion B: _____

Skills for Debate

Read and learn how to create effective supporting reasons.

How Can You Create Effective Supporting Reasons?

Along with explaining what, why, and how, you can formulate your supporting reasons by using two other methods. The first way is to focus on **why your argument is correct**. Discuss the advantages of your argument by outlining the benefits to individuals and society. You can also explain your point in terms of **cause-and-effect**. Explain the processes and events that occur as a result of your arguments. The second method is to **attack the opposing point of view**. Outline the problems that would occur in the opposite situation or mention flaws in the other team's line of reasoning.

Practicing Debate Skills

Read the debate motions and arguments below. Write the supporting reasons based on the types given for each argument.

1 **Debate Motion:** It is better for children to be homeschooled.
   Argument: Exceptionally bright students can learn more by being homeschooled.

Benefits of Your Argument | Cause-and-Effect

2 **Debate Motion:** Schoolteachers should be required to carry firearms.
   Argument: Arming teachers would make schools safer.

Problems with the Opposite Argument | Flaws in the Opposite Argument

Unit 06 B Debating the Topic

Creating Your Debate

Motion: It is better for students to attend single-sex schools.

What are your arguments? Get into two groups and plan for the debate. Decide whether your team is FOR (agree) or AGAINST (disagree) the motion. Then, create your ARE: Argument, Reason, and Example. Use the example arguments below and the research from your workbook to help create your arguments.

■ Example Arguments

FOR

Argument

Students can experience a more comfortable learning environment at single-sex schools.

Reason

Boys and girls have several major differences in terms of the way that they learn, socialize, and interact with other people. These differences can make students at coeducational schools feel uncomfortable being around members of the other sex.

Example

Professor Rosemary Salomone of St. John's University has stated, "Many students in single-sex classes report feeling more comfortable raising their hands and expressing uncertainty regarding a lesson or topic without fear of embarrassment or teasing from the opposite sex."

AGAINST

Argument

Students can learn how to interact with members of the opposite sex at coeducational schools.

Reason

In adult society, men and women interact with each other on a daily basis. The separation of genders at single-sex schools makes it almost impossible for students to learn about the other gender. This is a problem because children need to learn how to live with members of the opposite sex.

Example

The Institution of Education in London has found that men who attended boys' schools have a much greater chance of getting divorced since they did not learn how to interact with females as children.

Arguments FOR/AGAINST the Motion

ARGUMENT 1

Argument

Reason

Example

ARGUMENT 2

Argument

Reason

Example

ARGUMENT 3

Argument

Reason

Example

Actual Debate

Now, it's time to debate. Use the flow chart below to help you organize the debate.
The introductory expressions have been provided to help you. Put your arguments in logical order and make clear rebuttals to the opposing team's arguments.

Agree Opening Statement
We hold the belief that _____.

Agree Argument 1
For one, we contend that _____
_____
_____
_____.

Rebuttal 1
The problem with your argument is _____
_____.

Agree Argument 2
Let us next point out that _____
_____
_____.

Rebuttal 2
Despite your contention that _____
_____, we have to bring up the point that
_____
_____.

Agree Argument 3
The last argument we will make is _____
_____
_____.

Agree Closing Statement
To summarize, we assert that _____
_____
_____
_____.

Disagree Opening Statement
To us, there is no doubt that _____
_____.

Rebuttal 1
The flaw in the argument that _____
_____ is that
_____.

Disagree Argument 1
The first reason we believe that _____
_____
_____.

Rebuttal 2
Your second argument is unsound because
_____
_____.

Disagree Argument 2
To add to our first statement, _____
_____.

Rebuttal 3
Unfortunately, you have failed to consider that _____
_____.

Disagree Argument 3
To share our third argument, _____
_____.

Disagree Closing Statement
Overall, it is clear that _____
_____.

Sum Up the Debate

Finish the debate summary.

AGREEING SIDE'S ARGUMENT

Our debate today focused on the argument whether _____.

The first team expressed the belief that _____.

First, they claimed that _____.

The example that they gave was _____
_____.

The second point that they made was _____
_____
_____ was their supporting evidence.
_____ was their final point.

In detail, they explained that _____
_____.

DISAGREEING SIDE'S ARGUMENT

The second team felt differently. They explained that _____
_____.

The first argument that they made was _____
_____
_____ was the example they gave.

The team also felt that _____.

For instance, _____
_____.

The final point they made was that _____.

Specifically, they argued that _____
_____.

75

Chapter 4

Giving Supporting Examples

Unit 07 Celebrities Having No Right to Privacy

Unit 08 Replacing Textbooks with Tablets

Unit 07: Celebrities Having No Right to Privacy

WARM-UP

A. Discuss the following questions as a class.
1. What do you see in the picture above?
2. Why do you think the photographers are taking pictures of these people?
3. How do the people probably feel about having their pictures taken?

B. Answer the following questions with a partner.
1. Do you ever follow celebrity news and gossip? Why or why not?
2. Why is it important for the public to know about the personal lives of celebrities?
3. What are some situations where it might be inappropriate for the media to report about the lives of public figures?

Unit 07 A Learning about the Topic

Should the media scrutinize the private lives of famous people?

Read the passage and underline the main ideas. Track 19

The word "celebrity" has various meanings. It refers to a variety of people who directly shape society, including CEOs, politicians, movie stars, singers, and professional athletes. Being a celebrity requires one to use the media to spread a message about oneself. While most celebrities are completely willing to have the media cover their public lives, they often oppose media scrutiny of their private lives. Nevertheless, there are many advantages of allowing the media to report on the lives of public figures.

To start with, reporting on the lives of public figures keeps them honest and responsible. Famous people who act immorally or break the law should be publicly **disgraced**. This is what happened in 2009. Members of the British parliament in charge of making tax laws were discovered to have committed tax evasion. Afterward, many of these members **stepped down** from their positions. Second, distinguishing between the personal and public lives of celebrities is difficult. Most aspects of the lives of celebrities are exposed in the media. The events of their public lives frequently influence their private lives and **vice-versa**. Therefore, the public has a right to know about these events. As for the last point, the media publishes stories about celebrities since the public wants to know about them. Many of the bestselling newspapers are tabloids, which report on the personal lives of famous people.

Conversely, famous figures have as much right to privacy as the rest of us. Many people do not intend to become celebrities; they simply become well known because of their unique talents. For example, American professional basketball player Charles Barkley did not consider himself a role model and believed that the media should not scrutinize his private life. Another problem with excessive media coverage is the mental and physical **distress** it can cause famous people. Celebrities can suffer from stress and depression and may even die because of it. The most tragic instance is the death of Princess Diana in 1997. She died in a car crash while trying to escape the **paparazzi**. Finally, news coverage about the lives of celebrities reduces coverage of more important news events. Until the mid 20th century, the media largely reported on critical news stories. Today, around half of news reports focus on celebrity gossip. This makes it difficult for the public to learn about the news stories that matter.

Vocabulary Check

Choose the correct word for each definition.

| disgraced | step down | vice-versa | distress | paparazzo |

1 to give up a position; to resign
2 a photographer who takes and sells pictures of famous people
3 unhappiness or pain that affects the mind and body
4 feeling ashamed or embarrassed
5 used to show that an opposite statement is also true

Comprehension Questions

Check the correct answer for each question.

1 What makes it different to separate the personal and private lives of famous people?
- ☐ The fact that the events in their private lives affect their public lives
- ☐ The fact that most celebrities use the media to spread messages about themselves

2 Why does the media spend so much time writing stories about celebrities?
- ☐ Because the media has a responsibility to report on the people who influence our lives
- ☐ Because many people are interested in learning about celebrities' private lives

3 Why does the passage mention Princess Diana?
- ☐ To explain how media scrutiny harms the lives of celebrities
- ☐ To mention an important news story reported by the paparazzi

4 How has news reporting changed in recent decades?
- ☐ It has more coverage of stories that affect people's lives.
- ☐ It has a greater focus on reporting celebrity news stories.

Questions for Debate

Think of and share ideas to explore the debatable issues in the article. Be sure to state your opinion clearly and to provide one supporting idea for each opinion.

1. What types of news stories about famous people are often covered in the media? Are these important for people to know about?

   The news stories are usually about _____

   _____.

   As to whether they are important, I believe that _____

   _____.

2. Do you think it is possible for a person to be a celebrity while still having a private personal life?

   I believe that _____

   _____.

   To go into detail, _____

   _____.

3. Is it appropriate for the public to look up to celebrities as role models? Why or why not?

   My feeling about this is _____

   _____.

   This is due to the fact that _____

   _____.

4. In the past, the media did not report on the private lives of famous people, but it does today. What do you think has caused this change?

   This has probably changed because _____

   _____.

   For example, _____

   _____.

5. What would happen to news reporting if the media could not report on the lives of celebrities?

   The effect on the media would probably be _____

   _____.

   The impact of this is _____

   _____.

Opinion Examples

Look at the opinion examples about the motion below and answer the questions.

Motion: It is beneficial for the media to report on the lives of public figures.

Opinion A 🎧 Track 20

We should keep in mind that celebrities are still people and deserve to have as much privacy as anybody else. First, celebrities have personal problems that the world does not need to know about. A prominent example is former U.S. president Franklin Roosevelt. He was handicapped, but the media never reported on it at the time. Giving the public such information would have had no effect on his ability to be president. The media should also respect the privacy of celebrities because scrutiny of their lives gives them lots of stress. Celebrities today rarely have a moment's peace. This can cause them a lot of anxiety, which might make them depressed or angry.

Opinion B 🎧 Track 21

As far as I'm concerned, when people become famous, they give up their right to privacy. This is why the media examination of celebrities' private lives has to continue. One benefit is that it ensures that celebrities live up to their public roles. For example, the media should report on lawmakers who break the law themselves. Such hypocrites deserve to be shamed in public. Furthermore, the actions of celebrities in their private lives can influence their public lives. If a singer gets in a car accident, then he will not be able to perform for the public. In this case, the public should know about what happened to the singer in his private life.

1 Underline the main idea of each opinion.

2 Which opinion is for the topic? Which one is against it?
- FOR: _____
- AGAINST: _____

3 What supporting ideas does each opinion give?
- Opinion A: _____
- Opinion B: _____

4 Create one more supporting idea for each argument.
- Opinion A: _____
- Opinion B: _____

Skills for Debate

Read and learn how to create your examples.

How Should You Create Your Examples?

After giving your argument and supporting reasons, you must provide some **examples**. A strong example must **prove** your reasoning by describing **specific facts**, **situations**, and **events** which are **clearly related** to your argument. An example is relevant when it describes a **similar situation** to the ones you give in your arguments and reasons. In contrast, weak examples are **too general** or are **unrelated** to your arguments. Having strong examples is one of the keys to winning a debate, so be sure to create the best ones that you can.

Practicing Debate Skills

Read the following debate topic and its supporting arguments. Analyze the examples given for each argument and decide if they are strong or weak. If they are strong, explain why. If they are weak, rewrite them to make them stronger.

Sample Motion: Celebrities are poor role models for children.

1 Argument: Famous people often behave in ways that are immoral.

Example: The media always reports on celebrities behaving badly. These celebrities may act rudely toward others or do illegal activities. If children look up to famous people as role models, then they will likely imitate celebrities' bad behavior.

(☐ STRONG   ☐ WEAK)

→ _____

2 Argument: Looking up to famous people can motivate children to work toward greater personal goals.

Example: Oprah Winfrey is one of the most powerful media figures in the world today. However, she had to work hard to reach the top. She was born into poverty and was abused by her parents. Through her hard work, she became the host of her own talk show and now owns her own media corporation.

(☐ STRONG   ☐ WEAK)

→ _____

Unit 07 B Debating the Topic

Creating Your Debate

Motion: It is beneficial for the media to report on the lives of public figures.

What are your arguments? Get into two groups and plan for the debate. Decide whether your team is FOR (agree) or AGAINST (disagree) the motion. Then, create your ARE: Argument, Reason, and Example. Use the example arguments below and the research from your workbook to help create your arguments.

■ Example Arguments

FOR

Argument

The coverage of celebrities in the media gives people insight into the lives of these powerful figures.

Reason

Celebrities are people with great control over our lives. They influence our culture, language, and society. Reporting on their private lives enables normal people to understand these public figures better and to appreciate their social contributions.

Example

Many people consider the celebrity chef Gordon Ramsay to be rude and arrogant. However, reports about his private life shows that he is actually caring and considerate. These reports help the public to understand Ramsay better.

AGAINST

Argument

The coverage of celebrities' private lives takes time away from the reporting of more serious news stories.

Reason

A disproportionate amount of news coverage today is about the lives of celebrities. Less and less time is spent covering news stories that have relevance to people's lives. The problem with this is that people will be ignorant of issues that can affect them.

Example

A recent poll of Americans by Rasmussen Reports found that 87 percent of Americans believe that the media spends too much time covering celebrity gossip and scandals.

■ Arguments FOR/AGAINST the Motion

ARGUMENT 1

Argument

_____
_____
_____
_____
_____
_____

Reason

_____
_____
_____
_____
_____
_____

Example

_____
_____
_____
_____
_____
_____

ARGUMENT 2

Argument

_____
_____
_____
_____
_____
_____

Reason

_____
_____
_____
_____
_____
_____

Example

_____
_____
_____
_____
_____
_____

ARGUMENT 3

Argument

_____
_____
_____
_____
_____
_____

Reason

_____
_____
_____
_____
_____
_____

Example

_____
_____
_____
_____
_____
_____

Actual Debate

Now, it's time to debate. Use the flow chart below to help you organize the debate. The introductory expressions have been provided to help you. Put your arguments in logical order and make clear rebuttals to the opposing team's arguments.

Agree Opening Statement
Our team contends that it is entirely correct for _____.

Agree Argument 1
First, allow us to point out that _____.

Rebuttal 1
You have it completely wrong. The truth is that _____.

Agree Argument 2
To continue, we also reason that _____.

Rebuttal 2
We will rebut your argument by pointing out that _____.

Agree Argument 3
Our concluding argument is _____.

Agree Closing Statement
In summary, we hold on to the belief that _____.

Disagree Opening Statement
On the contrary, it is our assertion that _____.

Rebuttal 1
Your argument that _____ is flawed since _____.

Disagree Argument 1
Our opening argument is _____.

Rebuttal 2
Despite your supposition that _____, we contend that _____.

Disagree Argument 2
The next factor to consider is _____.

Rebuttal 3
To us, it is wrong to say that _____ because _____.

Disagree Argument 3
The final point we would like to mention is _____.

Disagree Closing Statement
The overall opinion of our team remains _____.

Sum Up the Debate

Finish the debate summary.

AGREEING SIDE'S ARGUMENT

Our debate topic today was _____.

The first team was in favor of the notion and claimed that _____.

First of all, _____.

More specifically, _____
_____.

Additionally, they posited that _____.

The reason that they felt this way was _____
_____.

Finally, they explained that _____.

To illustrate this, they mentioned that _____
_____.

DISAGREEING SIDE'S ARGUMENT

Unlike the first team, the second team argued that _____
_____.

Their opening argument was _____.

For instance, _____
_____.

To continue, they mentioned that _____.

The evidence that they provided was _____
_____.

_____ was their closing argument.

Their example was _____
_____.

Unit 08
Replacing Textbooks with Tablets

A. Discuss the following questions as a class.
1. What do you see in the picture above?
2. What do you think that the people are doing with their tablets?
3. Why might the man and the woman be smiling?

B. Answer the following questions with a partner.
1. What are some of the advantages that tablets have over textbooks?
2. Do you think that it would be easier to study by using a tablet? Why or why not?
3. How would schools benefit if they gave students tablets instead of textbooks?

Unit 08   A   Learning about the Topic

Should tablets take the place of textbooks in schools?

Read the passage and underline the main ideas. Track 22

We live in the digital age. Digital television has replaced analog television, MP3s have replaced records and cassettes, and email and text messages have taken the place of written letters. Due to this, it is logical for tablets and e-readers to replace textbooks in schools. Schools and students alike would benefit from such a change.

Most of all, tablets are much more convenient to use than books. Books are thick, heavy, and only carry a limited amount of content. In contrast, tablets are thin, light, and can hold vast amounts of information. A typical tablet with 8 gigabytes of memory could **store** 8,000 textbooks. Another advantage of tablets is that they can help students learn more efficiently. Tablets would allow teachers to give interactive lectures to students, which would make it easier to explain concepts to them. Students could also **scan** an entire textbook for a specific passage in less than a second. Finally, tablets would be far more cost effective in the long run. While textbooks have to be published and then shipped to schools, these expenses do not apply to digital readers. The tablet itself is expensive, but schools could purchase new books cheaply and get them immediately. One study estimates that **transitioning to** tablets would save American schools between $250 and $1,000 per student each year on textbook costs.

It is unlikely, though, that schools will **dispose of** their textbook collections anytime soon. For one, the upfront cost of purchasing tablets is great. One tablet costs about $300—the same price as several textbooks. While tablets are cheaper over a period of many years, the initial investment would be more than most schools could afford. Secondly, tablets would make it harder for students to read their texts. Multiple studies have found that people read printed text about 20 to 30 percent faster than they read the same words on a computer screen. For this reason, students would need to spend more hours studying from a tablet than they would studying from a textbook. Finally, tablets may serve as an **interruption** for students. Textbooks provide only academic content while tablets have many uses. Researchers have found that four-fifths of students also play games, send text messages, and surf the Internet on their tablets. This makes it harder for them to concentrate on their studies.

Vocabulary Check

Choose the correct word for each definition.

| store | scan | transition to | dispose of | interruption |

1 to look at something carefully to find something   _____
2 to throw away something; to get rid of something   _____
3 to keep something for later use   _____
4 to move from one thing to another   _____
5 an event that causes another event to stop happening   _____

Comprehension Questions

Check the correct answer for each question.

1 What are the primary reasons that tablets are more convenient to use than textbooks? Choose TWO correct answers.

   ☐ They are as thin as a single textbook.   ☐ They can hold more information.
   ☐ They need electricity to be used.   ☐ They can be used almost anywhere.

2 How could tablets be used to create lessons that are more informative for students?

   ☐ Students could search for information on a tablet and find it almost instantly.
   ☐ Teachers would be able to create lectures that students can participate in.

3 Why would tablets force students to spend more time studying?

   ☐ Because they would be distracted by the other features of the tablets
   ☐ Because they would have a harder time reading the text on the screen

4 What percentage of students use their tablets for purposes other than studying?

   ☐ 20 percent   ☐ 30 percent
   ☐ 60 percent   ☐ 80 percent

Questions for Debate

Think of and share ideas to explore the debatable issues in the article. Be sure to state your opinion clearly and to provide one supporting idea for each opinion.

1. What are some features of tablets that would enable students to study their texts more efficiently?

   Some of the features include _____

   _____.

   These would help students learn more because _____

   _____.

2. Would it be more cost effective for schools to give students textbooks or tablets? Explain.

   It seems to me that _____

   _____.

   The reason I feel this way is _____

   _____.

3. Do you believe that it is easier to read information from a textbook or a tablet? How would this affect a student's ability to study?

   I think that _____

   _____.

   This would affect students in terms of _____

   _____.

4. In what ways would tablets help teachers instruct students more effectively?

   Tablets would be beneficial in terms of _____

   _____.

   To go into detail, _____

   _____.

5. How could schools make sure that students are not distracted by the other features of tablets?

   Schools could _____

   _____.

   For example, _____

   _____.

Opinion Examples

Look at the opinion examples about the motion below and answer the questions.

Motion: Tablets should replace school textbooks.

Opinion A Track 23

Schools need to keep up with the times. They need to replace their textbooks with tablets. One benefit of tablets is that they are highly efficient. Tablets hold lots of information. A single tablet can easily store thousands of books. Even better, tablets can display audio and video, which help students learn more. On top of this, tablets can allow teachers to make interactive lectures. Teachers could have students answer questions on their tablets and see the students' answers in real time. This will allow teachers to measure what their students know and what they have trouble understanding. Then, they can change their lessons to enable their students to learn more.

Opinion B Track 24

As great a technology as tablets are, they are not a suitable replacement for textbooks. For starters, tablets distract students. Around 80 percent of students use their tablets to play games, to watch videos, and to browse the Internet. Conversely, when students learn from textbooks, there is nothing to distract them from their studies. Schools should also keep their textbooks because it is easier to study from printed books. Reading text printed on a computer screen is difficult. Researchers have found that people read computer text about 20 to 30 percent slower than the words in a printed book. The obvious problem is that students would have to spend more time studying. This is not an improvement.

1. Underline the main idea of each opinion.

2. Which opinion is for the topic? Which one is against it?
   - FOR: _____
   - AGAINST: _____

3. What supporting ideas does each opinion give?
   - Opinion A: _____
   - Opinion B: _____

4. Create one more supporting idea for each argument.
   - Opinion A: _____
   - Opinion B: _____

Skills for Debate

Read and learn how to introduce your points clearly.

How Should You Create Your Examples?

Many students prefer to make **personal experience** examples. These examples are based on the speakers' experiences. While this type of example is easy to create, other types of examples will support your argument more effectively. As you learned in the previous unit, effective examples center on **facts** and **research**. The examples that show this best are **statistics**, **expert opinions**, and **academic studies**. Statistics give percentages and numeric amounts to prove arguments. Expert opinions list the opinions of professors and other experts. Academic studies present research to support arguments.

Practicing Debate Skills

Read each of the following arguments below. Then, create examples according to the types given. Some phrases have been provided to help you.

Motion: Schools should require students to have their own laptops.

1 Argument: Laptops would make it easier for students to do their homework.

Idea Box

survey of 2,000 students / the majority completed their homework faster / search for information instantly

Example: *According to* _____

_____.

2 Argument: Laptops would present a major financial burden for many students.

Idea Box

one laptop costs several hundred dollars / many parents do not have extra money / cannot afford it

Example: *The truth of the matter is* _____

_____.

Unit 08 B Debating the Topic

Creating Your Debate

Motion: Tablets should replace school textbooks.

What are your arguments? Get into two groups and plan for the debate. Decide whether your team is FOR (agree) or AGAINST (disagree) the motion. Then, create your ARE: Argument, Reason, and Example. Use the example arguments below and the research from your workbook to help create your arguments.

■ Example Arguments

FOR	AGAINST
Argument	**Argument**
Tablets make learning more fun and interactive for students.	Schools cannot afford to buy tablets for all of their students.
Reason	**Reason**
Students today want to use technology as much as possible. Bringing tablets into the classroom will make students more interested in their studies. For this reason alone, students will learn more by using tablets.	While tablets would be cheaper in the end, their upfront cost is simply too much for schools to afford. They cannot get enough funding at one time to purchase tablets for every one of their students.
Example	**Example**
For instance, over 90 percent of students in one survey claimed that technology in the classroom helps them stay more interested in their studies.	The cost of one tablet can be $300 or greater. On the other hand, schools may only have to purchase one or two new books per student each year, which would be much cheaper.

Arguments FOR/AGAINST the Motion

ARGUMENT 1

Argument

___

Reason

___

Example

___

ARGUMENT 2

Argument

___

Reason

___

Example

___

ARGUMENT 3

Argument

___

Reason

___

Example

___

Actual Debate

Now, it's time to debate. Use the flow chart below to help you organize the debate.
The introductory expressions have been provided to help you. Put your arguments in logical order and make clear rebuttals to the opposing team's arguments.

Agree Opening Statement
We hold the firm conviction that _____.

Agree Argument 1
Our first argument is _____.

Rebuttal 1
You posit that _____. Yet we believe that _____.

Agree Argument 2
The second reason we support this idea is _____.

Rebuttal 2
You claimed that _____.
This is flawed because _____.

Agree Argument 3
Our last contention is _____.

Agree Closing Statement
On the whole, it is our conviction that _____.

Disagree Opening Statement
To us, it seems that it would be wrong to _____.

Rebuttal 1
That argument does not make sense. Think about _____.

Disagree Argument 1
The main reason that we oppose this motion is _____.

Rebuttal 2
It is wrong to say that _____ because _____.

Disagree Argument 2
Additionally, _____.

Rebuttal 3
The main falut in your third point is _____.

Disagree Argument 3
As for our final argument, _____.

Disagree Closing Statement
Our primary belief remains _____.

Sum Up the Debate

Finish the debate summary.

AGREEING SIDE'S ARGUMENT

Our debate topic today was _____.

The pro team agreed with the motion and posited that _____.

The first point that they made was _____.

The evidence that they offered was _____

_____.

Next, they claimed that _____.

To share their details, _____

_____.

Their final argument was _____.

For instance, _____

_____.

DISAGREEING SIDE'S ARGUMENT

The other team refuted the motion by claiming that _____

_____.

The first point they mentioned was _____.

_____

_____ was their supporting example.

They also claimed that _____.

The evidence that they offered was _____

_____.

Lastly, they stated that _____.

The support they gave was _____

_____.

Chapter 5

Doing Research

Unit 09 Fat Tax on Unhealthy Foods

Unit 10 Banning Homework at Schools

Unit 09 Fat Tax on Unhealthy Foods

A. Discuss the following questions as a class.

1. What do you see in the picture above?
2. Which foods in the picture are healthy? Which foods are unhealthy?
3. Do you think the man is healthy or unhealthy? Why do you think so?

B. Answer the following questions with a partner.

1. What foods do you think are unhealthy? List at least three of them.
2. How would a tax on unhealthy foods improve people's eating habits?
3. What are other products that the government places extra taxes on for the health of its citizens?

Unit 09 A Learning about the Topic

Should there be a fat tax on unhealthy foods?

Read the passage and underline the main ideas.  Track 25

As of today, nearly 1.5 billion adults around the world are overweight. Around 500 million of these people are obese, with a body-mass index (BMI) greater than 30. It is commonly known that the leading cause of weight gain is the excessive consumption of fat and calories. One proposed solution is to **implement** a fat tax. This would place a tax on food items that have very high levels of saturated fats, salt, and sugar. Only through a fat tax can governments improve people's eating habits.

Most notably, there are **precedents** for the creation of a fat tax. Governments the world over already have special taxes for other items considered unhealthy. Known as sin taxes, these are additional taxes placed upon items such as alcohol and cigarettes. A fat tax would likewise discourage people from eating unhealthy foods by raising their prices. Furthermore, obesity is not just a personal problem. Being overweight is known to lead to a number of serious health issues, including cancer, strokes, heart failure, back pain, and asthma. The World Health Organization (WHO) estimates that the United States wastes around $150 billion annually to treat health problems linked to being overweight. A final benefit of a fat tax is that it would equalize the cost between healthy and unhealthy foods. One of the main reasons that people turn to unhealthy processed foods is that they are much cheaper than fresh foods. A fat tax could be used to make fatty foods more expensive than fruits, vegetables, and other nutritious foods.

There remains doubt whether a fat tax could actually make people eat better. First of all, comparing a fat tax to sin taxes is flawed. Whereas sin taxes are put on **luxury** items—products which people consume for **pleasure**—a fat tax would raise the cost of food and thereby take away nutrition that people need for survival. Data also shows that a fat tax would do little to change people's eating habits. Junk foods are popular because they are tasty and convenient to eat. Even raising their prices by 20 percent is unlikely to stop people from eating them. Rather, it would be more effective to make healthy foods more accessible and to promote exercise. Lastly, a fat tax would **disproportionately** affect the lower classes. The poor often turn to processed foods because they cannot afford fresh foods. If the government makes these foods more expensive, then it will be taking away sources of nutrition from the most vulnerable members of society.

Vocabulary Check

Choose the correct word for each definition.

| implement | precedent | luxury | pleasure | disproportionately |

1. to make something active or effective
2. a feeling of happiness, enjoyment, or satisfaction
3. a similar action that happened at an earlier time
4. something that is expensive and not necessary
5. having a difference that is not fair to some groups of people

Comprehension Questions

Check the correct answer for each question.

1. What types of foods would be covered by a fat tax?
   - ☐ Foods that are the most popular among obese people
   - ☐ Foods that are high in saturated fats, salt, and sugar

2. What is the legal justification for the creation of a fat tax?
   - ☐ The fact that a fat tax would discourage people from eating unhealthy foods by raising their prices
   - ☐ The fact that the government places a sin tax on unhealthy items such as cigarettes

3. Why do people choose to eat unhealthy foods instead of fresh foods?
   - ☐ Because unhealthy foods are more convenient to buy than fresh foods
   - ☐ Because processed foods often cost less than fruits and vegetables

4. Which solutions would best encourage people to become healthier? Choose TWO correct answers.
   - ☐ Encouraging people to do physical activities
   - ☐ Producing foods that are convenient to eat
   - ☐ Raising junk food prices by 20 percent
   - ☐ Making healthy foods easier to obtain

Questions for Debate

Think of and share ideas to explore the debatable issues in the article. Be sure to state your opinion clearly and to provide one supporting idea for each opinion.

1. How many times a week do you eat unhealthy foods such as snacks and candy? Why?

   Each week, I eat unhealthy foods _____
   _____.

   I eat them this often because _____
   _____.

2. What are the main reasons that people choose to eat unhealthy foods?

   People probably eat unhealthy foods because _____
   _____.

   To share an example, _____
   _____.

3. Do you think the government has the right to restrict people's diets? Explain.

   My opinion about this is _____
   _____.

   I feel this way since _____
   _____.

4. How is a fat tax different from a sin tax on items such as cigarettes and alcohol?

   The difference between them is _____
   _____.

   This is important to note because _____
   _____.

5. Other than creating a fat tax, what are some effective ways that governments can improve their citizens' diets?

   Some other possible alternatives include _____
   _____.

   These could be more effective since _____
   _____.

Opinion Examples

Look at the opinion examples about the motion below and answer the questions.

> Motion: The government must create a fat tax for unhealthy foods.

Opinion A Track 26

More children and adults are obese today than in any other time in history. A fat tax can solve this. People mainly buy junk foods because they are cheaper than fresh foods. For example, Australian researchers determined that the prices of junk foods rise 20 percent less than the prices of healthy foods. A fat tax would make unhealthy foods so expensive that people would stop buying them. It is also necessary to point out that obesity is a problem that affects everyone. Overweight people are more likely to get sick. They often waste taxpayer money receiving medical treatment. The U.S. alone spends $150 billion a year treating health problems caused by obesity.

Opinion B Track 27

Living in a free society means having the right to do whatever you want as long as no one else suffers. The creation of a fat tax clearly violates this idea. Most notably, people must eat in order to survive. If governments create a fat tax, then they would make it more difficult for people to get the nutrition that they require. Besides, eating unhealthy foods does not guarantee that a person will become obese. Each day, millions of people eat fast food to save time and money, yet they are still healthy and of normal body weight. A fat tax would simply raise the cost of food without providing a solution for the obesity epidemic.

1 Underline the main idea of each opinion.

2 Which opinion is for the topic? Which one is against it?
- FOR: _____
- AGAINST: _____

3 What supporting ideas does each opinion give?
- Opinion A: _____
- Opinion B: _____

4 Create one more supporting idea for each argument.
- Opinion A: _____
- Opinion B: _____

Skills for Debate

Read and learn how to do your research.

How Should You Do Your Research?

A crucial component of creating effective debate arguments and examples is doing research. Most students today prefer to use **online search engines** such as Google to do their research. These search engines allow you to find articles relevant to your debate. Use specific **nouns** and **verbs** that describe your ideas. In addition, use terms such as "researcher," "professor," "statistics," and "personal experience" to help you find the information that you need to enhance your arguments. Another option is **online encyclopedias**. On these sites, search for articles that directly relate to your argument by using the key words from your debate motion. Then, use search terms to find the exact information that you need from each article.

Practicing Debate Skills

Think of the best key terms for researching each of the arguments below. Make sure that your key words are appropriate for each type of source. Some words have been provided to help you.

Motion: Lawmakers should restrict the amount of fat contained in food products.

1 It is the government's job to restrict people's unhealthy behavior.

Online Search Engine Key Words: lawmakers, junk foods, _____

Online Encyclopedia Key Words: fat content, fast foods, _____

2 Many fast-food products today contain dangerously high amounts of fat.

Online Search Engine Key Words: saturated fat, cheeseburger, _____

Online Encyclopedia Key Words: fast-food chains, unhealthy food, _____

Unit 09 B Debating the Topic

Creating Your Debate

Motion: The government must create a fat tax for unhealthy foods.

What are your arguments? Get into two groups and plan for the debate. Decide whether your team is FOR (agree) or AGAINST (disagree) the motion. Then, create your ARE: Argument, Reason, and Example. Use the example arguments below and the research from your workbook to help create your arguments.

▪ Example Arguments

FOR

Argument

Many food products today are dangerously unhealthy.

Reason

A number of fast-food products today contain huge amounts of fat and calories that are far more than people need to have. People who eat too many of these foods are likely to develop many serious health problems. A fat tax would discourage people from eating such unhealthy foods often.

Example

The Baskin-Robbins large Oreo Chocolate Shake contains 2,600 calories, 135 grams of fat, and 263 grams of sugar. This is equal to eating three healthy meals throughout the day.

AGAINST

Argument

People should have the right to eat whatever they want even if they become unhealthy.

Reason

Eating food is a personal choice. The government does not have the right to dictate what people may put into their bodies. However, the creation of a fat tax would severely restrict people's freedom of choice.

Example

To illustrate this point, consider purchasing a bicycle. The government does not tax people for buying bikes even though riding them can be very dangerous.

Arguments FOR/AGAINST the Motion

ARGUMENT 1

Argument

Reason

Example

ARGUMENT 2

Argument

Reason

Example

ARGUMENT 3

Argument

Reason

Example

Actual Debate

Now, it's time to debate. Use the flow chart below to help you organize the debate.
The introductory expressions have been provided to help you. Put your arguments in logical order and make clear rebuttals to the opposing team's arguments.

Agree Opening Statement
To our team, it is clear that _____
_____.

Agree Argument 1
To start with, _____
_____
_____
_____
_____.

Rebuttal 1
In spite of your assertion that _____
_____, we are certain that
_____.

Agree Argument 2
Second, consider that _____
_____
_____.

Rebuttal 2
Once again, you are mistaken. The reality is
_____
_____
_____.

Agree Argument 3
Finally, _____
_____
_____.

Agree Closing Statement
On the whole, it is obvious that _____
_____.

Disagree Opening Statement
Unlike our opponents, we feel that _____
_____.

Rebuttal 1
You are mistaken. The truth is _____
_____.

Disagree Argument 1
The first point we will make is _____
_____
_____.

Rebuttal 2
Your claim that _____
_____
is invalid because _____
_____.

Disagree Argument 2
Another point to keep in mind is _____
_____.

Rebuttal 3
Despite your opinion that _____
_____, it is our conviction that
_____.

Disagree Argument 3
One more point we will mention is _____
_____.

Disagree Closing Statement
In summation, it is evident that _____
_____.

Sum Up the Debate

Finish the debate summary.

AGREEING SIDE'S ARGUMENT

The topic of today's debate was _____.

The first team believed that _____.

For one, they claimed that _____.

The supporting details they provided included _____
_____.

Their next argument was _____.

Their evidence was _____
_____.

They concluded by mentioning that _____.
_____ was their example.

DISAGREEING SIDE'S ARGUMENT

Oppositely, it was the second team's opinion that _____
_____.

The first argument that they presented was _____.

For example, _____
_____.

Second of all, _____.

Their justification was _____
_____.

As for their final reason, it was _____.

Their rationale was _____
_____.

Unit 10
Banning Homework at Schools

A. Discuss the following questions as a class.
1. What do you see in the picture above?
2. What does the girl appear to be doing? How can you tell?
3. Do you think that the girl is enjoying herself? Why or why not?

B. Answer the following questions with a partner.
1. How much time do you spend doing homework each week? Do you think that this is an appropriate amount?
2. What are the primary ways that students would benefit from a homework ban?
3. What are the primary ways that teachers would benefit from a homework ban?

Unit 10 A Learning about the Topic

Should schools not be allowed to assign homework to students?

Read the passage and underline the main ideas.   Track 28

Does homework really help students learn? Many school administrators seem to think so. Schools have been giving students homework assignments for decades, and the amount of homework they give has continued to rise for more than twenty-five years. However, some lawmakers, educators, and parents have started to question the effectiveness of homework. Would students learn more if homework were banned altogether?

There are a number of reasons to remove homework from school curriculum. Above all, homework does little to help students learn more. When students do homework, they generally do it quickly and **carelessly**. As a result, they **retain** little information. For instance, students in Japan and Denmark receive little to no homework, yet their scores on international tests are among the highest in the world. Assigning homework also presents problems for teachers. Creating and checking homework assignments is a tiring, time-consuming process. The more time teachers spend on homework, the less time they have to prepare engaging class lessons, which has the greatest effect on student learning. As a result, homework is a **misuse** of teacher resources. We must also keep in mind that homework takes away time from students to do other activities. Schoolwork is important, but it is also necessary for children to be active in other ways. These can include practicing a musical instrument, participating on a sports team, or simply playing with their friends.

Even so, there are just as many persuasive reasons for schools to keep assigning homework to students. First, homework enables students to review and apply their schoolwork, gaining a **deeper** understanding of it. Professor Harris Cooper of Duke University determined that elementary school students who have regular homework assignments score higher on tests. Second, homework helps students learn to work independently. As adults, people need to be able to take initiative to solve problems and to meet deadlines on their own. If schools only require students to do schoolwork under the **guidance** of their teachers, then they will never develop independent work skills. A final point to consider is that homework allows students to learn more than they can in class alone. Schools only have a limited amount of time to cover lots of learning materials. Teachers must assign homework for their students to learn everything that they must. For instance, it is better to have students read novels and write essays as homework assignments than as class assignments.

Vocabulary Check

Choose the correct word for each definition.

| carelessly | retain | misuse | deep | guidance |

1 to use something incorrectly or inefficiently _____
2 to keep something in memory for a long time _____
3 help or advice that tells you what to do _____
4 having a great amount of content or knowledge _____
5 without thought or concern _____

Comprehension Questions

Check the correct answer for each question.

1 What is true about students in Japan and Denmark?
   ☐ They receive large amounts of homework.
   ☐ They have some of world's best test scores.

2 How does assigning homework misuse teacher resources?
   ☐ It forces teachers to create class lessons based on homework assignments.
   ☐ It makes it difficult for teachers to spend enough time creating interesting class activities.

3 Why do homework assignments enable students to better understand their lessons?
   ☐ Because students must make use of the information that they learn in school
   ☐ Because students will not waste time playing a musical instrument or team sports

4 What is the potential drawback of having students only do in-class assignments?
   ☐ They will be able to cover more learning materials by themselves.
   ☐ They will not develop the skills to work independently as adults.

Questions for Debate

Think of and share ideas to explore the debatable issues in the article. Be sure to state your opinion clearly and to provide one supporting idea for each opinion.

1. What types of assignments are appropriate to give students as homework?

    I believe that _____
    _____.

    The reason that I feel this way is _____
    _____.

2. How would teachers' lessons change if they could not assign homework?

    If homework were banned, then teachers would _____
    _____.

    To go into more detail, _____
    _____.

3. Is it possible for students to understand all of the materials that they study in class without help from their teachers? Explain.

    To me, it seems that _____
    _____.

    More specifically, _____
    _____.

4. How does having too many homework assignments negatively affect students' lives?

    When students have too much homework, then they _____
    _____.

    A clear example of this is _____
    _____.

5. Rather than banning homework, what are some other ways that schools could help students to learn more?

    Other solutions that may be more effective include _____
    _____.

    I think that this would work because _____
    _____.

Opinion Examples

Look at the opinion examples about the motion below and answer the questions.

Motion: School homework assignments should be banned.

Opinion A Track 29

While there are certainly drawbacks to assigning homework, it is not practical to ban it completely. For starters, think about all of the assignments that we don't have time to complete in class. Reading novels, writing essays, and making presentations all require lots of time. Teachers simply wouldn't be able to give students the time to do these assignments and to cover their lessons. Homework also gives students the chance to review the concepts that they learn about in class. It is rare that somebody can understand a new idea after one lesson. People need to be exposed to new concepts at least four times before they can grasp them. Homework lets students do that.

Opinion B Track 30

Teachers have been giving homework for decades, but does this mean it's right for them to do so? I don't think so. Doing homework is simply a waste of time for the majority of students. Chiefly, students don't focus on their homework. Many teachers only check to see that students complete their homework, not whether their answers are wrong or right. As a result, students often do their homework carelessly. Even worse, homework takes away time from other activities. Countless research has shown that students learn many important skills from playing, such as teamwork and problem solving. If students always have homework to do, then they can't ever develop these essential skills.

1 Underline the main idea of each opinion.

2 Which opinion is for the topic? Which one is against it?
- FOR: _____
- AGAINST: _____

3 What supporting ideas does each opinion give?
- Opinion A: _____
- Opinion B: _____

4 Create one more supporting idea for each argument.
- Opinion A: _____
- Opinion B: _____

Skills for Debate

Read and learn how to do your research.

How Should You Do Your Research?

When doing your research, you must decide which information you will include in your debate. To determine this, you must understand the difference between **relevant information** and **irrelevant information**. Relevant information directly supports your ideas and arguments with clear ideas and statistics. This includes **what action occurred**, who **it involves**, and **how it affects society**. On the contrary, irrelevant information does not support your argument. This includes minor details and arguments about different topics. Learning how to pick out the relevant facts is essential to doing effective research.

Practicing Debate Skills

Read the following arguments and their research. Determine if each research is relevant or irrelevant. If it is relevant, explain why. If it is irrelevant, rewrite it to make it relevant.

Motion: Teachers should be required to use technology in the classroom.

- **Argument 1:** Using technology in school will prepare students for the job market.

  Research: Nearly all middle-class white-collar jobs require applicants to have at least basic computer skills, including knowing how to use word processors and spreadsheets. **(RELEVANT / IRRELEVANT)**

- **Argument 2:** Technology in the classroom would only distract students from learning.

  Research: Researchers have recently discovered that over 90 percent of schools have computers in the classroom. **(RELEVANT / IRRELEVANT)**

Unit 10 B Debating the Topic

Creating Your Debate

Motion: School homework assignments should be banned.

What are your arguments? Get into two groups and plan for the debate. Decide whether your team is FOR (agree) or AGAINST (disagree) the motion. Then, create your ARE: Argument, Reason, and Example. Use the example arguments below and the research from your workbook to help create your arguments.

■ Example Arguments

FOR

Argument

Homework assignments have little effect on student academic achievement.

Reason

The majority of learning at school takes place in the classroom. Doing homework rarely teaches students new information and may actually confuse them about what they have learned. To learn effectively, students must study under the guidance of their teachers.

Example

For instance, students in Japan and Denmark have among the highest standardized test scores in the world. The reason is that they spend more time studying at school and almost no time doing homework.

AGAINST

Argument

Students need to do homework in order to review what they have learned about at school.

Reason

People, especially children, need to learn about a concept multiple times before they can master it. The benefit of homework is that children can review the material that they have learned and study it repeatedly until they fully understand.

Example

Research by Duke Professor Harris Cooper has revealed that elementary school students who have homework assignments have higher test scores than students who do not get homework.

Arguments FOR/AGAINST the Motion

ARGUMENT 1

Argument

Reason

Example

ARGUMENT 2

Argument

Reason

Example

ARGUMENT 3

Argument

Reason

Example

Actual Debate

Now, it's time to debate. Use the flow chart below to help you organize the debate.
The introductory expressions have been provided to help you. Put your arguments in logical order and make clear rebuttals to the opposing team's arguments.

Agree Opening Statement
We hold the firm conviction that _____.

Agree Argument 1
To start with, _____.

Rebuttal 1
It is a mistake to say that _____.

Agree Argument 2
Next, we must point out that _____.

Rebuttal 2
Your argument that _____ is wrong because _____.

Agree Argument 3
Our third assertion is _____.

Agree Closing Statement
The points that we have made clearly prove why _____.

Disagree Opening Statement
Conversely, from our perspective, it seems that _____.

Rebuttal 1
The main shortcoming of your argument that _____ is _____.

Disagree Argument 1
As for our first argument, it is _____.

Rebuttal 2
In spite of your supposition that _____, we contend that _____.

Disagree Argument 2
Another reason we disagree with this topic is _____.

Rebuttal 3
Your argument is flawed because _____.

Disagree Argument 3
Finally, _____.

Disagree Closing Statement
Ultimately, we feel that _____.

Sum Up the Debate

Finish the debate summary.

AGREEING SIDE'S ARGUMENT

Our debate today was about _____.

The opinion of the first team was _____.

They started by positing that _____.

For instance, _____

_____.

Additionally, _____.

To go into more detail, _____

_____.

Their final point was _____.

They offered _____

_____ as supporting evidence.

DISAGREEING SIDE'S ARGUMENT

To contradict the first team, the second team stated their belief that _____

_____

The first reason they opposed the motion was _____.

They gave the example of _____

_____.

Next, they posited that _____.

Their support was _____

_____.

To wrap up, they stated that _____.

_____

_____ was their reasoning.

Instilling Knowledge and Skills
for Thoughtful Debate

DEBATE Pro

Book 6

Jonathan S. McClelland

Workbook

DARAKWON

DEBATE Pro
Book 6

Workbook

Contents

How to Use This Book _4

Unit 01 Restricting Mass Tourism _6

Unit 02 Privatizing Education _10

Unit 03 Talking on Cell Phones on Public Transportation _14

Unit 04 Banning Bottled Water _18

Unit 05 Returning Art Stolen during Wars _22

Unit 06 Single-Gender Schools _26

Unit 07 Celebrities Having No Right to Privacy _30

Unit 08 Replacing Textbooks with Tablets _34

Unit 09 Fat Tax on Unhealthy Foods _38

Unit 10 Banning Homework at Schools _42

How to Use This Book

Overview

The workbook is intended to supplement the main book both during class and for homework. It provides space for students to take notes during class and to do additional research outside of class.

Introduction for each section

Organizing Ideas

This part requires students to analyze the reading passage from the main book and write down each of the arguments and examples for and against the topic.

Making Supporting Examples

This section helps students develop their skills in making examples. In each book, five types of examples are explained: statistics, expert opinions, facts, academic studies, and personal opinions.

Additional Research

This section provides students with additional information about the topic based on the type of example explained in the previous section. The information is followed by four brief comprehension questions. Sample phrases are provided to help students create their answers.

Your Research

In this section, students are asked to do additional research outside of class. They are encouraged to find information from magazines, newspapers, or academic websites and to write or tape the material in the space provided. Based on the information they find, students are asked to create four additional examples which they can use during their debate.

Debate Note-Taking

This section provides space which students can use to take notes during the debate.

Peer Evaluation

This part requires students to evaluate their peers' debate performance. Eight criteria are provided along with a ten-point scale for each criterion with a total maximum score of eighty points for each student.

Unit 01 Restricting Mass Tourism

Organizing Ideas

Should mass tourism be restricted in order to protect nature?

Look at the reading passage in your textbook. List all the supporting arguments both FOR and AGAINST. Then, add the supporting logic and examples for each argument.

FOR

Argument 1
_____
_____
_____

Support
_____
_____
_____

Argument 2
_____
_____
_____

Support
_____
_____
_____

Argument 3
_____
_____
_____

Support
_____
_____
_____

AGAINST

Argument 1
_____
_____
_____

Support
_____
_____
_____

Argument 2
_____
_____
_____

Support
_____
_____
_____

Argument 3
_____
_____
_____

Support
_____
_____
_____

Making Supporting Examples: Expert Opinions

Expert opinions are usually the ideas and opinions of experts in various fields. Experts are typically people such as professors, doctors, and business managers. Most experts base their opinions on their years of experience doing research and working in their fields. Below are some expert opinions related to the topic of restricting mass tourism.

Additional Research

Before starting your argument, let's do some extra research on the topic. Read the expert opinions about restricting mass tourism.

Dr. Janice Fong, Environmental Biologist
Almost no activity is worse for the environment than mass tourism. It brings thousands of people into contact with some of the most fragile environments on the planet. Without fail, this tourism damages these natural areas. The tourists themselves harm the environment by walking through forests, where they kill plants and animals along the way. Building tourist facilities such as hotels and restaurants alters the landscape and creates large-scale pollution. Tourism also requires large amounts of water, food, and energy resources. None of these problems would occur if tourism were banned.

Gunter Brown, Head of National Tourism
It is true that tourism harmed the environment in the past. This is no longer the case. Green tourism refers to the process of making tourism environmentally friendly. Tourists are educated on how to minimize their impact on the environment. They are taught not to leave any garbage behind and not to damage the environments that they visit. Tourist facilities are also becoming more environmentally friendly. The facilities are constructed by using local materials and building methods so as to disturb the environment as little as possible. And, of course, green technologies that reduce people's energy and water usage are employed throughout green tourist areas.

Work with a partner and answer the following questions. Phrases have been provided to help you.

1. According to Dr. Fong, why is mass tourism so harmful to the environment?
   → *She feels that it is so harmful because* _____.

2. How does building facilities for tourists harm the environment?
   → *It harms the environment in terms of* _____.

3. What does green tourism teach tourists to do?
   → *Green tourism teaches them to* _____.

4. Why are green tourist facilities more environmentally friendly?
   → *They are more environmentally friendly since* _____.

Your Research

Find an article about restricting mass tourism from a magazine, newspaper, or academic website. Paste or tape the article in your workbook in the space below.

Read your article and write four specific examples or pieces of evidence you can use for your debate. Try to include different types of examples, including opinion polls, statistics, academic studies, and general facts.

-
-
-
-

Debate Note-Taking

Use this page to take notes about the opposing team's arguments during the debate.

Note-Taking

Peer Evaluation

Read the assessment criteria and objectively evaluate your peers on a scale from 1 to 10.

CRITERIA	Name				
Understands the subject well	/10	/10	/10	/10	/10
Supports opinion with clear logic and examples	/10	/10	/10	/10	/10
Introduces opinions with appropriate connectors (In my view, I agree, For example, etc.)	/10	/10	/10	/10	/10
Uses a variety of vocabulary and expressions	/10	/10	/10	/10	/10
Accurately uses a variety of grammatical structures	/10	/10	/10	/10	/10
Does not monopolize the conversation and lets other people express themselves	/10	/10	/10	/10	/10
Listens attentively and respects other people's opinions	/10	/10	/10	/10	/10
Is able to accept criticism without becoming upset	/10	/10	/10	/10	/10
TOTAL SCORE	/80	/80	/80	/80	/80

Unit 02: Privatizing Education

Organizing Ideas

Should all formal education be made private?

Look at the reading passage in your textbook. List all the supporting arguments both FOR and AGAINST. Then, add the supporting logic and examples for each argument.

FOR

Argument 1

Support

Argument 2

Support

Argument 3

Support

AGAINST

Argument 1

Support

Argument 2

Support

Argument 3

Support

Making Supporting Examples: Academic Studies

Academic studies are research that is done by universities, governments, and large research organizations. During these studies, researchers examine events to understand what causes them and why they are important. Using academic studies is a good way to strengthen your argument. Below are some academic studies related to the topic of privatizing education.

Additional Research

Before starting your argument, let's do some extra research on the topic. Read the academic studies about privatizing education.

> As a way to correct the shortcomings of public education, a number of people are coming out in support of private education. To determine whether private schools offer students a better education, our research team evaluated these schools across several different metrics. Our results call into question the idea that private education is superior to public schools.
>
> **Private Schools May Not Lead to Higher Test Scores**
> Many supporters of private education point to the supposedly higher test scores that are a direct result of private education. However, the difference in scores may be attributed in large part to the admissions process of private schools. To be admitted to many private schools, incoming students must have grades and test scores that are already higher than average. This suggests that test scores at private schools are higher because the students at these schools are above average in the first place.
>
> **Parental Social Status a Main Factor for Success**
> Another often overlooked factor when evaluating the quality of private schools is the typical social status of the parents who enroll their children in private schools. Children whose parents earn more money generally do better at school. Their parents tend to be more educated themselves and place a greater emphasis on studying and academic achievement. The parents of most private school students earn more than $75,000 a year and have at least a four-year college degree.

Work with a partner and answer the following questions. Phrases have been provided to help you.

1. What is the main conclusion of the researchers?
   → *The researchers mainly believe that* _____.

2. Why are private school students' test scores higher on average?
   → *Their scores are probably higher because* _____.

3. How does the social status of children's parents affect their academic performance?
   → *Generally speaking,* _____.

4. What is true about most parents of students at private schools?
   → *These parents usually* _____.

Your Research

Find an article about privatizing education from a magazine, newspaper, or academic website. Paste or tape the article in your workbook in the space below.

Read your article and write four specific examples or pieces of evidence you can use for your debate. Try to include different types of examples, including opinion polls, statistics, academic studies, and general facts.

-
-
-
-

Debate Note-Taking

Use this page to take notes about the opposing team's arguments during the debate.

Note-Taking

Peer Evaluation

Read the assessment criteria and objectively evaluate your peers on a scale from 1 to 10.

CRITERIA	Name				
Understands the subject well	/10	/10	/10	/10	/10
Supports opinion with clear logic and examples	/10	/10	/10	/10	/10
Introduces opinions with appropriate connectors (In my view, I agree, For example, etc.)	/10	/10	/10	/10	/10
Uses a variety of vocabulary and expressions	/10	/10	/10	/10	/10
Accurately uses a variety of grammatical structures	/10	/10	/10	/10	/10
Does not monopolize the conversation and lets other people express themselves	/10	/10	/10	/10	/10
Listens attentively and respects other people's opinions	/10	/10	/10	/10	/10
Is able to accept criticism without becoming upset	/10	/10	/10	/10	/10
TOTAL SCORE	/80	/80	/80	/80	/80

Unit 03: Talking on Cell Phones on Public Transportation

Organizing Ideas

Should people not be allowed to talk on thier cell phones on public transportation?

Look at the reading passage in your textbook. List all the supporting arguments both FOR and AGAINST. Then, add the supporting logic and examples for each argument.

FOR	AGAINST
Argument 1	**Argument 1**
Support	**Support**
Argument 2	**Argument 2**
Support	**Support**
Argument 3	**Argument 3**
Support	**Support**

Making Supporting Examples: Personal Experience

Personal experience is your experience related to the topic. Using personal experience can be a good way to support your argument if you explain how your experience proves your point. However, you should be careful because one person's experience might not be common. This can actually weaken your argument. Below are some personal experiences related to the topic of talking on cell phones on public transportation.

Additional Research

Before starting your argument, let's do some extra research on the topic. Read the personal experiences about talking on cell phones on public transportation.

Joseph Moss, Businessman

I take the bus and subway to work each day. To get all of my work done, talking on my cell phone is essential. While riding on public transportation, I use my phone to discuss work issues, to arrange meetings, and to schedule appointments with my coworkers and clients. This means that when I arrive at the office, I can concentrate on tasks that are more important and get more work done. If I couldn't talk on my cell phone on public transportation, then it would be much harder for me to finish all of my work on time. So, as far as I'm concerned, people should definitely be allowed to talk on their phones on buses and subways.

Karen Cooper, Designer

Fortunately, I don't have to ride on public transportation too often. But when I do ride it, I'm always annoyed when some passengers use their cell phones to call other people. For one, people often have loud, inappropriate conversations on their phones. They talk about personal subjects that make me and other passengers feel uncomfortable. People's phones seem to make them forget that they're in a public place. Likewise, people cannot easily get away from others who are talking on their cell phones. It's often difficult for people to move to another car or to get another seat. This means that they are forced to listen to conversations that they don't want to hear.

Work with a partner and answer the following questions. Phrases have been provided to help you.

1 What are the ways that Joseph uses his cell phone on public transportation?

→ He mainly uses his cell phone to _____.

2 How would Joseph's work be affected if he could not use his phone on public transportation?

→ His work would _____.

3 According to Karen, why do people have inappropriate conversations on their cell phones?

→ Karen believes that _____.

4 Why are passengers often forced to listen to other people's conversations on public transportation?

→ They are forced to listen because _____.

Your Research

Find an article about talking on cell phones on public transportation from a magazine, newspaper, or academic website. Paste or tape the article in your workbook in the space below.

Paste or Tape Your Research Article Here

Read your article and write four specific examples or pieces of evidence you can use for your debate. Try to include different types of examples, including opinion polls, statistics, academic studies, and general facts.

- _____
- _____
- _____
- _____

Debate Note-Taking

Use this page to take notes about the opposing team's arguments during the debate.

Note-Taking

Peer Evaluation

Read the assessment criteria and objectively evaluate your peers on a scale from 1 to 10.

CRITERIA	Name				
Understands the subject well	/10	/10	/10	/10	/10
Supports opinion with clear logic and examples	/10	/10	/10	/10	/10
Introduces opinions with appropriate connectors (In my view, I agree, For example, etc.)	/10	/10	/10	/10	/10
Uses a variety of vocabulary and expressions	/10	/10	/10	/10	/10
Accurately uses a variety of grammatical structures	/10	/10	/10	/10	/10
Does not monopolize the conversation and lets other people express themselves	/10	/10	/10	/10	/10
Listens attentively and respects other people's opinions	/10	/10	/10	/10	/10
Is able to accept criticism without becoming upset	/10	/10	/10	/10	/10
TOTAL SCORE	/80	/80	/80	/80	/80

Unit 04 Banning Bottled Water

Organizing Ideas

Should people stop drinking bottled water?

Look at the reading passage in your textbook. List all the supporting arguments both FOR and AGAINST. Then, add the supporting logic and examples for each argument.

FOR	AGAINST
Argument 1	**Argument 1**
Support	**Support**
Argument 2	**Argument 2**
Support	**Support**
Argument 3	**Argument 3**
Support	**Support**

Making Supporting Examples: Statistics

Statistics are facts based on numbers. They are usually created by governments, universities, news organizations, and companies. Statistics often show the number of people, companies, and nations that agree with a certain opinion or policy. To show these numbers, statistics can include percentages, populations, and points. Below are some statistics related to the topic of banning bottled water.

Additional Research

Before starting your argument, let's do some extra research on the topic. Read the statistics about banning bottled water.

> Drinking bottled water may be trendy these days, but that does not mean that you should do it. The five statistics below will make you think twice about buying bottled water.
>
> 1. **Making Bottled Water Consumes 17 Million Barrels of Oil Each Year**
>   Producing the plastic for water bottles requires huge amounts of electricity. The 17 million barrels annually used to make water bottles would be enough to power one million cars for an entire year.
>
> 2. **80 Percent of Water Bottles Are Never Recycled**
>   Even though water bottles are designed to be easily recycled, the majority of them end up in landfills after they are used.
>
> 3. **Producing a Water Bottle Requires Three Times More Water than the Bottle Holds**
>   The plastic-making process uses far more water than each bottle can actually contain.
>
> 4. **Over Half of Bottled Water Is Simply Tap Water**
>   Nearly all of the bottled water sold by Coca-Cola and Pepsi is tap water taken from local supplies.
>
> 5. **Bottled Water Is 75 Times More Expensive than Tap Water**
>   A two-liter bottle of water can cost a $1.50 or more compared to the $0.02 needed to buy the same amount of tap water.

Work with a partner and answer the following questions. Phrases have been provided to help you.

1 What is the number of cars that can be powered by the amount of oil used to make plastic bottles annually?

→ *The number of cars is* _____.

2 How much water is required to produce one plastic water bottle?

→ *The amount of water that is required is* _____.

3 *Where does the majority of bottled water come from?*

→ *Most bottled water* _____.

4 What is the price of two liters of bottled water? How does this compare to the price of tap water?

→ *A two-liter bottle of water costs* _____ *while two liters of tap water is* _____.

Your Research

Find an article about banning bottled water from a magazine, newspaper, or academic website. Paste or tape the article in your workbook in the space below.

Paste or Tape Your Research Article Here

Read your article and write four specific examples or pieces of evidence you can use for your debate. Try to include different types of examples, including opinion polls, statistics, academic studies, and general facts.

- _____
- _____
- _____
- _____

Debate Note-Taking

Use this page to take notes about the opposing team's arguments during the debate.

Note-Taking

___

Peer Evaluation

Read the assessment criteria and objectively evaluate your peers on a scale from 1 to 10.

CRITERIA	Name				
Understands the subject well	/10	/10	/10	/10	/10
Supports opinion with clear logic and examples	/10	/10	/10	/10	/10
Introduces opinions with appropriate connectors (In my view, I agree, For example, etc.)	/10	/10	/10	/10	/10
Uses a variety of vocabulary and expressions	/10	/10	/10	/10	/10
Accurately uses a variety of grammatical structures	/10	/10	/10	/10	/10
Does not monopolize the conversation and lets other people express themselves	/10	/10	/10	/10	/10
Listens attentively and respects other people's opinions	/10	/10	/10	/10	/10
Is able to accept criticism without becoming upset	/10	/10	/10	/10	/10
TOTAL SCORE	/80	/80	/80	/80	/80

Unit 05 Returning Art Stolen during Wars

Organizing Ideas

Should artwork stolen during wars be returned to its home countries?

Look at the reading passage in your textbook. List all the supporting arguments both FOR and AGAINST. Then, add the supporting logic and examples for each argument.

FOR	AGAINST
Argument 1	**Argument 1**
Support	**Support**
Argument 2	**Argument 2**
Support	**Support**
Argument 3	**Argument 3**
Support	**Support**

Making Supporting Examples: Facts

A fact is something true. For debates, you can use facts that are common knowledge, but you should also try to use more specific, less commonly known facts. The best places to find specific facts are newspaper and magazine articles. In these sources, you can find all of the details of a situation and can read interviews from people related to the story. Below are some facts related to the topic of returning artwork stolen during wars.

Additional Research

Before starting your argument, let's do some extra research on the topic. Read the facts about returning art stolen during wars.

> Nearly all nations agree that the works of art looted by the Germans during World War II should be returned to their home nations. Unfortunately, the scale of the problem and the lack of clear laws regarding looted artwork make it difficult to ensure that the stolen pieces are returned to their lawful owners. Consider the following facts:
> - Approximately 100,000 pieces of artwork stolen by the Germans during World War II remain missing. Most of these missing works are believed to be in the possession of private collectors.
> - German law has a 30-year statute of limitation. Since the Second World War ended over 70 years ago, the rightful owners of the stolen works have no legal right to demand the return of their pieces.
> - In 1998, the Washington Principles were adopted by 44 countries. The plan identifies and resolves claims for stolen art. However, the agreement does not legally require the owners of stolen artwork to return the pieces.

Work with a partner and answer the following questions. Phrases have been provided to help you.

1 What are the main reasons that it is difficult to return stolen artwork to its proper owners?
→ *The reasons are* _____.

2 Where is most of the looted artwork believed to be kept?
→ *It is believed that most of the missing artwork is* _____
_____.

3 Why is there no legal course of action for the owners of looted art to get their pieces back?
→ *The owners have no legal course of action because* _____
_____.

4 How effective is the Washington Principles at helping looted artwork be returned?
→ *The Washington Principles are* _____
_____.

Your Research

Find an article about returning art stolen during wars from a magazine, newspaper, or academic website. Paste or tape the article in your workbook in the space below.

Paste or Tape Your Research Article Here

Read your article and write four specific examples or pieces of evidence you can use for your debate. Try to include different types of examples, including opinion polls, statistics, academic studies, and general facts.

-
-
-
-

Debate Note-Taking

Use this page to take notes about the opposing team's arguments during the debate.

Note-Taking

Peer Evaluation

Read the assessment criteria and objectively evaluate your peers on a scale from 1 to 10.

CRITERIA	Name				
Understands the subject well	/10	/10	/10	/10	/10
Supports opinion with clear logic and examples	/10	/10	/10	/10	/10
Introduces opinions with appropriate connectors (In my view, I agree, For example, etc.)	/10	/10	/10	/10	/10
Uses a variety of vocabulary and expressions	/10	/10	/10	/10	/10
Accurately uses a variety of grammatical structures	/10	/10	/10	/10	/10
Does not monopolize the conversation and lets other people express themselves	/10	/10	/10	/10	/10
Listens attentively and respects other people's opinions	/10	/10	/10	/10	/10
Is able to accept criticism without becoming upset	/10	/10	/10	/10	/10
TOTAL SCORE	/80	/80	/80	/80	/80

Unit 06 Single-Gender Schools

Organizing Ideas

Should all schools be single gender only?

Look at the reading passage in your textbook. List all the supporting arguments both FOR and AGAINST. Then, add the supporting logic and examples for each argument.

FOR

Argument 1

Support

Argument 2

Support

Argument 3

Support

AGAINST

Argument 1

Support

Argument 2

Support

Argument 3

Support

Making Supporting Examples: Personal Experience

Personal experience is your experience related to the topic. Using personal experience can be a good way to support your argument if you explain how your experience proves your point. However, you should be careful because one person's experience might not be common. This can actually weaken your argument. Below are some personal experiences related to the topic of single-gender schools.

Additional Research

Before starting your argument, let's do some extra research on the topic. Read the personal experiences about single-gender schools.

Monica Pratt, Canadian Middle School Student

This year, I'm going to an all-girls school, and it's great. Coming here has helped me understand all of the problems co-ed schools have. The boys always tried to show off in front of the girls, and the girls spent a lot of time trying to look pretty for the boys. So not many of the students were concerned about their studies. When we were in class, the boys loved doing hands-on projects while the girls preferred having class discussions. This difference in the ways that boys and girls learn made it hard for all of the students to learn equally well.

Seth Yin, Taiwanese Middle School Student

My school has both boys and girls, and I don't see anything wrong with it. Sure, sometimes the boys and girls don't get along very well, but that teaches us how to overcome and understand our differences. If I just went to a boy's school, I would probably never know how girls think and act. In any case, mixed schools show us what the real world is like. Look at most jobs that adults have. They almost never work only with men or women. Men and women have to work together. At my co-ed school, I have to learn how to work with girls even if we learn in different ways.

Work with a partner and answer the following questions. Phrases have been provided to help you.

1. Why did the students at Monica's coeducational school not focus on their schoolwork?

   → *The students did not focus because* _____.

2. According to Monica, what class activities do boys learn better from, and what activities do girls learn better from?

   → *She says that boys prefer* _____ *whereas girls like* _____.

3. Why does Seth think that it is not a problem that boys and girls are not always friendly to each other?

   → *He thinks that it is not a problem since* _____.

4. According to Seth, how do co-ed schools better prepare students for the real world?

   → *They prepare students better because* _____.

Your Research

Find an article about single-gender schools from a magazine, newspaper, or academic website. Paste or tape the article in your workbook in the space below.

Paste or Tape Your Research Article Here

Read your article and write four specific examples or pieces of evidence you can use for your debate. Try to include different types of examples, including opinion polls, statistics, academic studies, and general facts.

- _____
- _____
- _____
- _____

Debate Note-Taking

Use this page to take notes about the opposing team's arguments during the debate.

Note-Taking

Peer Evaluation

Read the assessment criteria and objectively evaluate your peers on a scale from 1 to 10.

CRITERIA	Name				
Understands the subject well	/10	/10	/10	/10	/10
Supports opinion with clear logic and examples	/10	/10	/10	/10	/10
Introduces opinions with appropriate connectors (In my view, I agree, For example, etc.)	/10	/10	/10	/10	/10
Uses a variety of vocabulary and expressions	/10	/10	/10	/10	/10
Accurately uses a variety of grammatical structures	/10	/10	/10	/10	/10
Does not monopolize the conversation and lets other people express themselves	/10	/10	/10	/10	/10
Listens attentively and respects other people's opinions	/10	/10	/10	/10	/10
Is able to accept criticism without becoming upset	/10	/10	/10	/10	/10
TOTAL SCORE	/80	/80	/80	/80	/80

Unit 07 Celebrities Having No Right to Privacy

Organizing Ideas

Should the media scrutinize the private lives of famous people?

Look at the reading passage in your textbook. List all the supporting arguments both FOR and AGAINST. Then, add the supporting logic and examples for each argument.

FOR

Argument 1
_____
_____
_____

Support
_____
_____

Argument 2
_____
_____
_____

Support
_____
_____

Argument 3
_____
_____
_____

Support
_____
_____

AGAINST

Argument 1
_____
_____
_____

Support
_____
_____

Argument 2
_____
_____
_____

Support
_____
_____

Argument 3
_____
_____
_____

Support
_____
_____

Making Supporting Examples: Facts

A fact is something true. For debates, you can use facts that are common knowledge, but you should also try to use more specific, less commonly known facts. The best places to find specific facts are newspaper and magazine articles. In these sources, you can find all of the details of a situation and can read interviews from people related to the story. Below are some facts related to the topic of celebrities having no right to privacy.

Additional Research

Before starting your argument, let's do some extra research on the topic. Read the facts about celebrities having no right to privacy.

> The U.S. Constitution does not clearly define a right to personal privacy. Nevertheless, the courts have recognized the rights of celebrities to privacy. The most influential article on the subject is a *Harvard Law Review* article entitled "The Right to Privacy." The article outlines the following types of invasions of privacy:
>
> 1. Intrusion into solitude – where reporters invade a person's private time
> 2. Disclosure of private facts to the public – where reporters expose private information to the public
> 3. Misrepresentation of a private individual – where reporters make false statements about a person
> 4. Commercial exploitation of a person's image – where reporters use a person's identity for their personal benefit
>
> The best-known case of a celebrity successfully restricting the actions of celebrity photographers is *Galella versus Onassis*. Jacqueline Kennedy Onassis brought action against photographer Ron Galella for his constant photography of her and her children. Although the court ruled that Mr. Galella had a right to photograph Ms. Onassis and her children, he was not allowed to come within 10 meters of them at any time. Despite the precedent of the *Galella versus Onassis* case, few celebrities have used it to protect their own privacy.

Work with a partner and answer the following questions. Phrases have been provided to help you.

1 Which article defined rights to personal privacy? Who was it written by?

→ The name of the article is _____, and it was written by _____.

2 What is an example of commercial exploitation of a person's image?

→ A good example would be _____.

3 What was the outcome in the case of *Galella versus Onassis*?

→ The outcome of the case was _____.

4 How have celebrities made use of the *Galella versus Onassis* case?

→ Most celebrities have _____.

Your Research

Find an article about celebrities having no right to privacy from a magazine, newspaper, or academic website. Paste or tape the article in your workbook in the space below.

Paste or Tape Your Research Article Here

Read your article and write four specific examples or pieces of evidence you can use for your debate. Try to include different types of examples, including opinion polls, statistics, academic studies, and general facts.

- _____
- _____
- _____
- _____

Debate Note-Taking

Use this page to take notes about the opposing team's arguments during the debate.

Note-Taking

Peer Evaluation

Read the assessment criteria and objectively evaluate your peers on a scale from 1 to 10.

CRITERIA	Name				
Understands the subject well	/10	/10	/10	/10	/10
Supports opinion with clear logic and examples	/10	/10	/10	/10	/10
Introduces opinions with appropriate connectors (In my view, I agree, For example, etc.)	/10	/10	/10	/10	/10
Uses a variety of vocabulary and expressions	/10	/10	/10	/10	/10
Accurately uses a variety of grammatical structures	/10	/10	/10	/10	/10
Does not monopolize the conversation and lets other people express themselves	/10	/10	/10	/10	/10
Listens attentively and respects other people's opinions	/10	/10	/10	/10	/10
Is able to accept criticism without becoming upset	/10	/10	/10	/10	/10
TOTAL SCORE	/80	/80	/80	/80	/80

Unit 08: Replacing Textbooks with Tablets

Organizing Ideas

Should tablets take the place of textbooks in schools?

Look at the reading passage in your textbook. List all the supporting arguments both FOR and AGAINST. Then, add the supporting logic and examples for each argument.

FOR	AGAINST
Argument 1	**Argument 1**
Support	**Support**
Argument 2	**Argument 2**
Support	**Support**
Argument 3	**Argument 3**
Support	**Support**

Making Supporting Examples: Statistics

Statistics are facts based on numbers. They are usually created by governments, universities, news organizations, and companies. Statistics often show the number of people, companies, and nations that agree with a certain opinion or policy. To show these numbers, statistics can include percentages, populations, and points. Below are some statistics related to the topic of replacing textbooks with tablets.

Additional Research

Before starting your argument, let's do some extra research on the topic. Read the statistics about replacing textbooks with tablets.

Tablets are an amazing technology. Some people feel that tablets should replace textbooks in the classroom, but should they? Here are some statistics to help you decide.

Number of Books Contained

Just one tablet can hold eight thousand or more textbooks. An old-fashioned textbook contains just one book. Even better, teachers can use tablets to show students educational videos in class. This means that students can learn far more from tablets than they can learn from textbooks.

Total Cost after 12 Years of Schooling

One tablet costs about $300, roughly three times the price of one textbook. Even so, over the span of a student's academic career, a tablet is much cheaper than all of the textbooks the student needs. The main reason is that schools can download new textbooks to tablets for around $10 per book. Compared to paper textbooks, which must be printed and shipped to schools, digital textbooks are far less expensive in the long term.

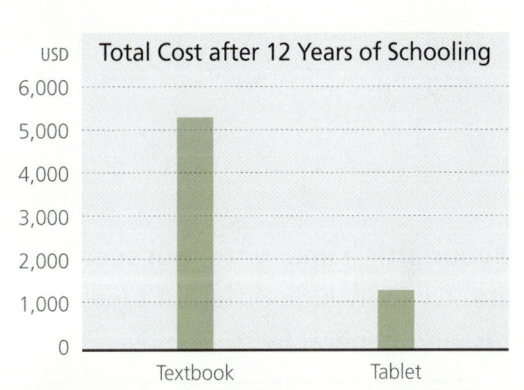

Work with a partner and answer the following questions. Phrases have been provided to help you.

1 How many books can tablets contain compared to traditional textbooks?

→ *Tablets can contain* _____ *compared to textbooks, which hold* _____ .

2 Aside from holding textbooks, what other information can tablets store?

→ *Tablets can also* _____ .

3 How much does a tablet cost compared to a textbook?

→ *Compared to a textbook, a tablet* _____ .

4 Why would schools save money on tablets in the long run?

→ *Schools would save money since* _____ .

Your Research

Find an article about replacing textbooks with tablets from a magazine, newspaper, or academic website. Paste or tape the article in your workbook in the space below.

Paste or Tape Your Research Article Here

Read your article and write four specific examples or pieces of evidence you can use for your debate. Try to include different types of examples, including opinion polls, statistics, academic studies, and general facts.

-
-
-
-

Debate Note-Taking

Use this page to take notes about the opposing team's arguments during the debate.

Note-Taking

Peer Evaluation

Read the assessment criteria and objectively evaluate your peers on a scale from 1 to 10.

CRITERIA	Name				
Understands the subject well	/10	/10	/10	/10	/10
Supports opinion with clear logic and examples	/10	/10	/10	/10	/10
Introduces opinions with appropriate connectors (In my view, I agree, For example, etc.)	/10	/10	/10	/10	/10
Uses a variety of vocabulary and expressions	/10	/10	/10	/10	/10
Accurately uses a variety of grammatical structures	/10	/10	/10	/10	/10
Does not monopolize the conversation and lets other people express themselves	/10	/10	/10	/10	/10
Listens attentively and respects other people's opinions	/10	/10	/10	/10	/10
Is able to accept criticism without becoming upset	/10	/10	/10	/10	/10
TOTAL SCORE	/80	/80	/80	/80	/80

Unit 09: Fat Tax on Unhealthy Foods

Organizing Ideas

Should there be a fat tax on unhealthy foods?

Look at the reading passage in your textbook. List all the supporting arguments both FOR and AGAINST. Then, add the supporting logic and examples for each argument.

FOR	AGAINST
Argument 1	**Argument 1**
Support	**Support**
Argument 2	**Argument 2**
Support	**Support**
Argument 3	**Argument 3**
Support	**Support**

Making Supporting Examples: Academic Studies

Academic studies are research that is done by universities, governments, and large research organizations. During these studies, researchers examine events to understand what causes them and why they are important. Using academic studies is a good way to strengthen your argument. Below are some academic studies related to the topic of a fat tax on unhealthy foods.

Additional Research

Before starting your argument, let's do some extra research on the topic. Read the academic studies about a fat tax on unhealthy foods.

> In the past few decades, the number of unhealthy foods available has exploded. Most of these foods are processed foods and fast foods, which contain an extremely excessive amount of fat and calories. These foods present a real danger to the public, and this is why the implementation of a fat tax is necessary. Just read these shocking truths about today's unhealthy foods.
>
> - Fast foods today contain extremely high levels of saturated fats and calories. A countless number of meals at fast-food restaurants include over 2,500 calories and more than 80 grams of fat, the amounts recommended for an entire day's worth of food for adults.
>
> - Governments have placed a "sin tax" on unhealthy items such as cigarettes and alcohol for decades. Their reason for doing this is to make these products too expensive for people to purchase and consume whenever they want.
>
> - Healthy foods are 10 times more expensive than unhealthy foods. The cost of 2,000 calories of junk food is roughly $3.50. On the contrary, getting the same amount of calories from healthy food would cost over $36 dollars. A fat tax would go a long way to correcting this price difference.

Work with a partner and answer the following questions. Phrases have been provided to help you.

1 What type of food has become much more popular in recent years? Why is this a problem?

→ The type of food is _____, which is a problem since _____.

2 What is significant about 2,500 calories and 80 grams of fat?

→ These numbers are significant because _____.

3 How do sin taxes affect people's purchasing habits?

→ The purpose of sin taxes is _____.

4 What is the price difference between healthy and unhealthy foods? How would a fat tax improve this situation?

→ The difference in price is _____.

Your Research

Find an article about a fat tax on unhealthy foods from a magazine, newspaper, or academic website. Paste or tape the article in your workbook in the space below.

Paste or Tape Your Research Article Here

Read your article and write four specific examples or pieces of evidence you can use for your debate. Try to include different types of examples, including opinion polls, statistics, academic studies, and general facts.

-
-
-
-

Debate Note-Taking

Use this page to take notes about the opposing team's arguments during the debate.

Note-Taking

Peer Evaluation

Read the assessment criteria and objectively evaluate your peers on a scale from 1 to 10.

CRITERIA	Name				
Understands the subject well	/10	/10	/10	/10	/10
Supports opinion with clear logic and examples	/10	/10	/10	/10	/10
Introduces opinions with appropriate connectors (In my view, I agree, For example, etc.)	/10	/10	/10	/10	/10
Uses a variety of vocabulary and expressions	/10	/10	/10	/10	/10
Accurately uses a variety of grammatical structures	/10	/10	/10	/10	/10
Does not monopolize the conversation and lets other people express themselves	/10	/10	/10	/10	/10
Listens attentively and respects other people's opinions	/10	/10	/10	/10	/10
Is able to accept criticism without becoming upset	/10	/10	/10	/10	/10
TOTAL SCORE	/80	/80	/80	/80	/80

Unit 10 Banning Homework at Schools

Organizing Ideas

Should schools not be allowed to assign homework to students?

Look at the reading passage in your textbook. List all the supporting arguments both FOR and AGAINST. Then, add the supporting logic and examples for each argument.

FOR	AGAINST
Argument 1	**Argument 1**
Support	**Support**
Argument 2	**Argument 2**
Support	**Support**
Argument 3	**Argument 3**
Support	**Support**

Making Supporting Examples: Expert Opinions

Expert opinions are usually the ideas and opinions of experts in various fields. Experts are typically people such as professors, doctors, and business managers. Most experts base their opinions on their years of experience doing research and working in their fields. Below are some expert opinions related to the topic of banning homework in schools.

Additional Research

Before starting your argument, let's do some extra research on the topic. Read the expert opinion about banning homework in schools.

Dr. Ryan Kerry, Superintendent of Seattle Public Schools

As the superintendent of public schools in Seattle, part of my duty is to improve the curriculum and learning methods used at my schools. One of the main changes that I am proposing is the elimination of daily homework assignments. I am confident that such a change will help the students at Seattle's schools learn better.

Doing daily homework assignments negatively affects students. A large body of evidence indicates that students learn the best under the guidance of a teacher. Teachers can help them to understand concepts and ideas that they could not figure out on their own. The same studies have suggested that students who do not understand their homework material will learn it incorrectly. It takes teachers more time to teach students how to unlearn their incorrect methods and understand the correct methods than it does to teach students how to solve problems the right way the first time.

Homework also brings about serious difficulties for teachers. Each day, teachers must spend their precious time creating and checking homework assignments. This gives teachers less time and energy to develop lessons that are more engaging for students. What ends up happening is that teachers do not teach students well in the first place, so they give students homework assignments that they do not properly understand. Therefore, it would be far more effective to let teachers develop better class materials so that students can learn properly in school, which would make homework assignments unnecessary.

Work with a partner and answer the following questions. Phrases have been provided to help you.

1 What is beneficial about studying with a teacher?

→ *It is beneficial in terms of* _____.

2 How can homework cause students to learn information incorrectly?

→ *Homework can* _____.

3 In what way does homework lead to poor lessons from teachers?

→ *It can result in* _____.

4 If homework were banned, how would it affect teachers' work?

→ *Banning homework would* _____.

Your Research

Find an article about banning homework in schools from a magazine, newspaper, or academic website. Paste or tape the article in your workbook in the space below.

Paste or Tape Your Research Article Here

Read your article and write four specific examples or pieces of evidence you can use for your debate. Try to include different types of examples, including opinion polls, statistics, academic studies, and general facts.

- _____
- _____
- _____
- _____

Debate Note-Taking

Use this page to take notes about the opposing team's arguments during the debate.

Note-Taking

_____

Peer Evaluation

Read the assessment criteria and objectively evaluate your peers on a scale from 1 to 10.

CRITERIA	Name				
Understands the subject well	/10	/10	/10	/10	/10
Supports opinion with clear logic and examples	/10	/10	/10	/10	/10
Introduces opinions with appropriate connectors (In my view, I agree, For example, etc.)	/10	/10	/10	/10	/10
Uses a variety of vocabulary and expressions	/10	/10	/10	/10	/10
Accurately uses a variety of grammatical structures	/10	/10	/10	/10	/10
Does not monopolize the conversation and lets other people express themselves	/10	/10	/10	/10	/10
Listens attentively and respects other people's opinions	/10	/10	/10	/10	/10
Is able to accept criticism without becoming upset	/10	/10	/10	/10	/10
TOTAL SCORE	/80	/80	/80	/80	/80

Memo

Memo

DEBATE Pro
Book 6
Workbook